ANTHROPOLOGICAL PAPERS OF
THE UNIVERSITY OF ARIZONA
NUMBER 16

# LITHIC ANALYSIS AND CULTURAL INFERENCE

A Paleo-Indian Case

EDWIN N. WILMSEN

THE UNIVERSITY OF ARIZONA PRESS
TUCSON, ARIZONA 1970

*Second printing 1973*
*First printing 1970*

THE UNIVERSITY OF ARIZONA PRESS

Copyright © 1970
The Arizona Board of Regents
All Rights Reserved
Manufactured in the U.S.A.

S.B.N. 8165-0211-0
L.C. No. 75-89880

*For My Parents*

# PREFACE

This study is founded upon the notion that the archaeological record of any given time and place is the record of the operation of cultural events at that time and place. Motivation for anthropological study of such a record stems from the desire to elucidate as fully as these data permit the underlying cultural significance of that record. There are, of course, other motivations for interest in archaeology—delight in the aesthetic quality of objects; desire to catalogue historical events; curiosity about the capabilities of one's antecedents. These are all legitimate concerns; however, the position taken here is that only through an anthropological approach may we hope to arrive at an understanding of the processes which molded the events behind the fossil record.

The search for such understanding requires procedures that are radically different from those commonly employed by archaeologists in the past. Fortunately, such procedures are being developed. Technical methods for handling data and modes of thought by which these data may be interpreted are being adapted from other disciplines. More importantly, anthropological methodology is itself undergoing rapid change; the traditional collection of impressionistic devices for handling data is being replaced with a more systematically constructed body of rules for observing and interpreting cultural phenomena.

This study forms part of this effort to construct a more formalized system for handling cultural data. Specifically, it presents a number of methods whereby lithic artifacts may be described and classified. Some suggestions are advanced for the use of these methods in defining intra-cultural uniformities in assemblages of such materials and for the identification, ultimately, of cross-cultural regularities in lithic inventories. An attempt is made to identify systematic relationships between variables in the technical and social spheres of culture. Such an attempt, if successful, can lead to a deeper understanding of cultural processes. An explanation of these processes is the ultimate goal of anthropological research. This study may contribute to the realization of this goal.

A great many people have helped to make this study a reality. First among these are the members of my dissertation committee, Emil W. Haury, William A. Longacre, and Raymond H. Thompson. Each has contributed differently, but importantly, to the development of this work. Others who have read all or parts of the manuscript are: Lewis R. Binford, Sally R. Binford, Edward P. Dozier, Bernard Fontana, Kenneth L. Hale, James J. Hester, Paul S. Martin, Albert C. Spaulding, Edward H. Spicer, and Richard B. Woodbury.

This study would have been impossible without the generous cooperation of a number of repository institutions and collection owners who gave me free access to their collections. My debt to each of these is specifically recorded in the section in which the collections are described.

A large part of my graduate work, of which this monograph is the culmination, was supported by a National Science Foundation Graduate Fellowship. This study was specifically supported by a National Science Foundation Dissertation Improvement Grant. I am pleased to record my gratitude for this support. The Smithsonian Institution, through its Predoctoral Internship Program, provided funds and facilities for a major part of this study. The entire staff of the Smithsonian Office of Anthropology, together with members of other divisions of the Institution, was more than unselfish in assisting me in countless ways. Richard B. Woodbury, then chairman of the Office of Anthropology, played a masterful role in supervising my work at the Institution, giving me all the rope that I could get tangled up in but not quite so much that I could hang myself. I had the opportunity to make an earlier study of this kind supported by the American Philosophical Society and a National Science Foundation Institutional Grant at the University of Arizona.

The data presented here were processed on an IBM 7027 computer in the Numerical Analysis Laboratory, University of Arizona. Mrs. Janet Beauchamp programmed the data. I am especially grateful to Lucien Duckstein, Department of Systems Engineering, for his advice in the statistical portions of this work.

Finally, my wife, Susan, deserves special mention for her constant encouragement and frequent help in seeing this work to completion. My children have been a constant source of inspiration and have acted variously as secretaries, bibliographers, and data recorders.

# CONTENTS

|     |                                          | Page |
| --- | ---------------------------------------- | ---- |
|     | **ABSTRACT**                             | xi   |
| 1.  | **INTRODUCTION**                         | 1    |
| 2.  | **A CULTURAL FRAMEWORK**                 | 2    |
|     | Cultural Structure                       | 2    |
|     | Cultural Variation                       | 3    |
|     | Cultural Units                           | 3    |
| 3.  | **ARCHAEOLOGICAL SYSTEMATICS**           | 5    |
|     | Sampling                                 | 5    |
|     | Description                              | 6    |
|     | Classification                           | 6    |
| 4.  | **PROCEDURES**                           | 8    |
|     | Site Selection                           | 8    |
|     | Sample Selection                         | 8    |
|     | Definition of Variables                  | 10   |
| 5.  | **THE DATA**                             | 22   |
|     | Sources of Data                          | 22   |
|     |     Blackwater       | 22   |
|     |     Quad             | 22   |
|     |     Shoop            | 22   |
|     |     Williamson       | 23   |
|     |     Lindenmeier      | 23   |
|     |     Vernon           | 23   |
|     |     Levi             | 23   |
|     |     Horner           | 24   |
|     |     Denbigh          | 24   |
|     |     Big Kiokee Creek | 24   |
|     | Description of the Data                  | 24   |
|     |     Material         | 25   |
|     |     Striking Platform Characteristics | 27 |

|     |     |     |
| --- | --- | --- |
|     | Flake Angle | 27 |
|     | The Medial Axis | 31 |
|     | Artifact Dimensions | 31 |
|     | Edge Angles | 37 |
|     | Correlations between Variables | 42 |
|     | Comparisons between Samples | 51 |
|     | Tool Categories | 51 |
|     | Artifact Population Sites | 62 |
| 6.  | **PROCESSES OF ARTIFACT PRODUCTION** | 66 |
|     | Raw Material Selection | 66 |
|     | Technological Variation | 66 |
|     | Functional Variation | 68 |
| 7.  | **SITE ACTIVITIES** | 75 |
|     | Lindenmeier | 75 |
|     | Quad | 76 |
|     | Levi | 77 |
|     | Blackwater | 78 |
|     | Horner | 79 |
|     | Shoop | 79 |
|     | Williamson | 79 |
|     | Vernon | 80 |
| 8.  | **STRUCTURE IN PALEO-INDIAN CULTURE** | 81 |
|     | Localization of Paleo-Indian Groups | 81 |
|     | Social Integration | 82 |
|     | Subsistence and Task Performance | 82 |
|     | **REFERENCES** | 84 |

# LIST OF ILLUSTRATIONS

| | | |
|---|---|---|
| Figure 1. | Location of Sites | 9 |
| Figure 2. | Code Key | 12 |
| Figure 3. | Platform Preparation and Dimensions | 15 |
| Figure 4. | Platform Abrasion | 16 |
| Figure 5. | Flake Angle ($< \beta$) Measurements | 17 |
| Figure 6. | Medial Axis ($< \alpha$) Measurements | 18 |
| Figure 7. | Flake Dimensions | 19 |

| | | |
|---|---|---|
| Figure 8. | Notation for Retouch Position | 20 |
| Figure 9. | Lateral Edge ($<\delta_L$) Measurement | 21 |
| Figure 10. | Distal Edge ($<\delta_D$) Measurement | 21 |
| Figure 11. | Proportional Frequency Distributions of $<\beta$ for Lindenmeier and Blackwater | 29 |
| Figure 12. | Proportional Frequency Distributions of $<\beta$ for Horner and Levi | 29 |
| Figure 13. | Proportional Frequency Distributions of $<\beta$ for Shoop and Williamson | 30 |
| Figure 14. | Proportional Frequency Distributions of $<\beta$ for Quad and Vernon | 30 |
| Figure 15. | Proportional Frequency Distributions of $<\alpha$ for Lindenmeier, Blackwater, Horner, and Levi | 32 |
| Figure 16. | Proportional Frequency Distributions of $<\alpha$ for Shoop, Williamson, Quad, and Vernon | 33 |
| Figure 17. | Proportional Frequency Distribution of $<\delta_L$ and $<\delta_D$ for Lindenmeier | 38 |
| Figure 18. | Proportional Frequency Distribution of $<\delta_L$ and $<\delta_D$ for Blackwater | 38 |
| Figure 19. | Proportional Frequency Distribution of $<\delta_L$ and $<\delta_D$ for Horner | 39 |
| Figure 20. | Proportional Frequency Distribution of $<\delta_L$ and $<\delta_D$ for Levi | 39 |
| Figure 21. | Proportional Frequency Distribution of $<\delta_L$ and $<\delta_D$ for Shoop | 40 |
| Figure 22. | Proportional Frequency Distribution of $<\delta_L$ and $<\delta_D$ for Williamson | 40 |
| Figure 23. | Proportional Frequency Distribution of $<\delta_L$ and $<\delta_D$ for Quad | 41 |
| Figure 24. | Proportional Freuqnecy Distribution of $<\delta_L$ and $<\delta_D$ for Vernon | 41 |
| Figure 25. | Formal Categories I - IV | 57 |
| Figure 26. | Formal Categories V - VII | 58 |
| Figure 27. | Formal Categories VIII - IX | 59 |
| Figure 28. | Formal Categories X - XI | 60 |
| Figure 29. | Formal Categories XII - XIII | 61 |
| Figure 30. | Frequency Distributions of $<\beta$ and $<\alpha$ for Denbigh and Big Kiokee Creek | 69 |
| Figure 31. | Wear Patterns on Stone Tools | 72 |

# LIST OF TABLES

| | | |
|---|---|---|
| Table 1. | Chronology of Sites | 10 |
| Table 2. | Assemblage and Sample Sizes | 11 |
| Table 3. | Proportional Frequencies of Raw Materials and Flake Types | 26 |
| Table 4. | Striking Platform Characteristics | 28 |
| Table 5. | Mean Values of Length (mm) and Width-Length Ratios | 34 |
| Table 6. | Mean Values of Width (mm) and Frequency of Incidence of Maximum Width Position Values | 35 |

| | | |
|---|---|---|
| Table 7. | Mean Values of Thickness (mm) and Thickness Ratios | 36 |
| Table 8. | Edge Angle Values and Frequency of Accessory Tool Forms | 42 |
| Table 9. | Correlations between Variables: Pooled Data | 43 |
| Table 10. | Correlations between Variables: Lindenmeier | 44 |
| Table 11. | Correlations between Variables: Horner | 45 |
| Table 12. | Correlations between Variables: Levi | 46 |
| Table 13. | Correlations between Variables: Williamson | 47 |
| Table 14. | Correlations between Variables: Quad | 48 |
| Table 15. | Correlations between Variables: Vernon | 49 |
| Table 16. | Between Sample Comparisons of $t$ | 52 |
| Table 17. | Between Sample Comparisons of $<\beta$ | 52 |
| Table 18. | Between Sample Comparisons of $<\alpha$ | 53 |
| Table 19. | Between Sample Comparisons of $L$ | 53 |
| Table 20. | Between Sample Comparisons of $W$ | 54 |
| Table 21. | Between Sample Comparisons of $T$ | 54 |
| Table 22. | Between Sample Comparisons of $<\delta_L$ | 55 |
| Table 23. | Between Sample Comparisons of $<\delta_D$ | 55 |
| Table 24. | Distributions of Tool Categories within Samples | 63 |
| Table 25. | Distributions of Associated Artifacts and Non-artifactual remains | 64 |
| Table 26. | Test Scores of Significance ($t$) between Site Flake Characteristics | 70 |

# ABSTRACT

Within a theoretical framework which attempts to treat archaeological data as the remains of extinct cultural systems, a methodology for analyzing stone inventories is here presented. Data from eight sites—Lindenmeier, Blackwater, Horner, Levi, Shoop, Williamson, Quad, Vernon—are utilized to exemplify the method.

Some basic requirements of a cultural theory which can incorporate archaeological data are enumerated. It is suggested that such a theory will be general and formal and that it will generate mechanisms for recognizing the structure, the internal variation, and the constituent units of cultural systems. It is argued that methods for describing cultural data must serve the needs of the general theory and that both the presence and the extent of artifact variation must be systematically determined. A number of procedures for statistically describing artifact inventories are introduced. The extent of mutual covariation between quantitative variables within inventories and between site assemblages is tested. These procedures are discussed in detail. Data are presented in both textual and graphic form. A set of thirteen formal tool categories is derived from the data. The facts of individual tool variation are subsumed within these general categories. It is argued that, within a systematic descriptive procedure, the generalities of formal tool morphology are of primary interest and that the elucidation of cultural processes depends upon the recognition of those common elements that underlie individual variations in form and meaning.

Inferences concerning the processes of artifact production are drawn directly from the data. It is suggested that technological control of artifact production was well developed and that immediately useful artifacts were economically produced. Intersite variation in artifact morphology is seen to be related to intersite variations in functional activities. More abstractly, a number of inferences about the nature of Paleo-Indian social and cultural life are advanced. It is suggested that Paleo-Indians were not dependent solely upon the hunting of Pleistocene megafauna and that much evidence of a wide range of cultural activities exists. These activities are discussed in some detail.

# 1. INTRODUCTION

Archaeologists as anthropologists are concerned with the problem of discovering those fundamental, underlying properties of cultural processes that are common to extinct as well as to living cultural systems. It is this interest that weds archaeology to those other segments of anthropology which seek cultural explanation. Archaeologists must assume that, other things being equal, those processes which structure the ethnographic record have also structured the archaeological record. When ecological conditions, sociocultural integration, or primary subsistence patterns similar to those known ethnographically can be demonstrated or inferred archaeologically, the archaeologist must orient his investigation toward the elucidation of those processual factors which may underlie both ethnographic and archaeological cases and he must seek structural explanations for the similarities and differences that are recognized.

Recently, a number of archaeologists have realized that, in order to achieve their anthropological goals, new procedures for the collection, description, and interpretation of archaeological data must be formulated within a general theoretical framework in which explanatory inferences may be tested against the whole range of anthropological data.

Most models of culture fail to yield mechanisms by which hypotheses of uniform process operation and systemic cultural structure may be tested in archaeological contexts. They fail to provide satisfactory and uniformly useful procedures which allow data from a number of sources to be evaluated against each other.

Clearly, a theoretical structure is needed that will incorporate archaeological data in a general anthropological framework. Such a theory will permit a series of hypotheses to be generated for testing against known sets of facts gathered in field work. It will provide, furthermore, a set of criteria that will permit rejection of any given model by the demonstration of counter-examples. On an elementary level, this will allow archaeologists to confidently assign artifacts to proper classes. It is not only the obvious classes (e.g. fluted as opposed to non-fluted projectile point classes) that can be treated so, but also the more obscure classes (e.g. classes of unmodified stone flakes). On an explanatory level, a model will express the structural relationships among the observed data and will permit us to predict new phenomena by constructing general laws of cultural processes. In order to provide a background to the proposals presented herein, it will be necessary to enumerate superficially some of the more obvious constituents of such a theory.

In the next chapter, certain requirements of a holistic cultural theory are examined and some suggestions advanced toward meeting these requirements. This is followed by a consideration of a systematic methodology directed toward the identification, classification, and explanation of archaeological data within the context established in chapter two. Next, a system for describing lithic material and for identifying systematic attribute articulations is introduced. Data from a number of collections are utilized to exemplify the method. In subsequent chapters, a series of inferences drawn from these data is developed and some suggestions for testing these inferences are offered.

# 2. A CULTURAL FRAMEWORK

Any theory of culture, to be useful in a meaningful way, must apply equally to all segments of the cultural record. It must fit the paleolithic case as well as the modern industrial case. This requirement imposes the condition of generality upon the theory. Notions of culture that are bound by category restrictions cannot be productive in any systematic sense, for they are overly concerned with definitions that equate culture with material object clusters, idea frames, social forms, values, and the like. This circumscribed viewpoint imposes unacceptable limits upon cultural theory and effectively prevents inferences drawn from data in one category (e.g. ethnographically-derived information about social forms) from being applied to data in any other category (e.g. archaeologically-derived information about material objects). The resultant restrictions upon archaeological inference are obvious. An adequate theory of culture must permit inferences concerning the nature of cultural processes to be drawn from the materials of extinct cultural systems as well as from the direct observation of living societies.

A second condition which must be imposed upon the theory is that of formality. Only a formal theory can provide precise mechanisms for the evaluation of data. Loose formulations and intuitive constructions are by their nature vague and invariably lead to ambiguous interpretations. They do not provide determinative criteria for agreement on such matters as the classification and interpretation of data. Systematic explanation is precluded by such theories.

If either of these conditions is relaxed—conditions which are common to all general theories—there will be no way to choose among alternate proposals each of which may be compatible with some particular set of field data but none of which reveal the underlying cultural structure of any case. In addition, a theory of culture must meet certain conditions specific to itself. Some of these specific conditions are enumerated below. Later in this chapter it will be argued that any theory which fails to meet *all* of these conditions of adequacy will fail to be useful in the search for explanation of cultural processes.

## CULTURAL STRUCTURE

Initially, any theory of culture must recognize the systemic structure of culture. One possible way of meeting this condition, the one adopted here, is to view culture as the system of adaptive mechanisms with which the member units of human society integrate with their environments. This, of course, is not an original view. Radcliffe-Brown (1933: ix), in what may have been the original statement of such a position, advocated a "conception of culture as an adaptive mechanism by which a certain number of human beings are enabled to live a social life as an ordered community in an environment." Childe (1936), too, was concerned with the relationship of culture to environment, but he seemed to regard culture as a result of, rather than as an agent for, adaptation. More recently, White (1959b) considered the adaptive nature of culture and Sahlins and Service (1960) have examined some of the mechanics of cultural-environmental interaction.

Environment is here taken to include both the natural and the social elements in an ecological setting. Since neither the natural nor the social elements of environments are constants, it follows that there will be different forms of interaction in space and time between cultural systems and environments. These adaptive processes will lead to integrative processes that strengthen the social cohesion of a group and make more effective the cultural articulation of that group with its environment. These integrative processes, in turn, open new adaptive possibilities or limit further adaptation. We may designate any particular form of this interaction *a culture* if we can isolate a specific subset of these adaptive mechanisms that is demonstrably distinct from other such identifiable subsets and that is articulated by a particular social group. Binford (1965: 205) has espoused a similar view. Any theory of culture, if it is to be archaeologically useful, must recognize the adaptive nature of cultural systems and must express cultural structure in terms of interrelationships among ideas, objects, and social forms.

## CULTURAL VARIATION

We may expand upon this notion by observing that a cultural system is traditionally derived by virtue of the fact that individuals draw upon a cultural reservoir which is common to overlapping generations of participants in the system and that in large measure each individual intuitively constructs his own cultural framework through his participation in the system. Consider, however, that idiosyncracies in participation experience and inherited ability, as well as non-cultural variables introduced by environmental irregularity, will generate slightly differing behavior sequences within any given cultural system.

Individuals participate in culture by interacting with environments. In doing so, they select from among those behavior sequences with which they are familiar and initiate those appropriate to a given situation. Furthermore, since individual participation is within a cultural reference system held in common with other members of a society, behavior sequences will tend to vary within the limits of that system. This is a familiar aspect of systems. Individuals who are in frequent intimate contact will draw upon a common set of culture referents in the form of idea frames, object clusters, motor syndromes, and social forms. A common referent system generates structured behavior sequences that can be observed ethnographically and that leave structured records amenable to systematic archaeological analysis.

Archaeologists, in concert with other anthropologists, are developing methodologies that will permit them to distinguish between the superficial appearance and the underlying structure of any aggregate of cultural events. On a low level of analysis, statistical procedures are useful in making such distinctions. For higher levels of interpretation and explanation, procedures for recognizing general patterns and universal structural regularities must be developed.

## CULTURAL UNITS

In a preliminary way, we may define cultural units as those with which a society encounters and manipulates its environment. This statement is compatible with a view of culture as an adaptive system; it does not, however, clarify the relationship between cultural and social units. If these are equivalent units, no useful distinction can be made between the broader concepts "culture" and "society". I would suggest that there are strong reasons for assuming qualitative differences between different forms of cultural units and that social units comprise only one set of forms isolatable from among those that cultural units may take. Radcliffe-Brown (1933: ix) recognized a distinction between the internal relations of individuals within the social unity, and the external relations of the society to its environment. He urged the study of cultures as adaptive and integrative systems with subsequent comparison of as many variant systems as possible. Service (1962) has offered a consideration of the adaptive nature of cultural systems.

It is apparent that some cultural units may be isolated with respect to their internal cohesion in social relations only. But these social units must be integrated with their environments through the operation of qualitatively different structural poses—those which integrate people with things and ideas. Gearing (1962: 15) has defined a structural pose as "the way a simple human society [is] appropriately organized at a particular moment for a particular purpose." He has also said that individuals in a social group recurrently move into and out of relationships with other members of the group (Gearing 1958: 1154). It is apparent, furthermore, that individual participation in different structural poses fluctuates in response to differential functional needs. Vayda (1966) has suggested that the structural poses of a society are controlled by environmental factors, the degree of isolation of the society, the availability of personnel, and differential task performance requirements.

Compare, for example, the operation of a simple nuclear family in its internal and external poses. As a social unit, the family structures the interpersonal relations of its members both within the family and with the members of other ingroup social units. In its other poses, the family relates its members' economic, political, and ideological activities to ecological conditions of resource availability and competitor activity. In assigning cultural positions to individuals, any cultural unit considers such factors as ability, experience, and prestige as well as social position.

These observations apply equally to very simple levels of sociocultural integration as well as to higher levels. We may draw an illustration from Steward's Basin Shoshonean-family level. Whether this level is the product of aboriginal adjustment to a limited environment as Steward (1938; 1955) maintains or is due to post-contact adjustment to European encroachments as argued by Service (1962) is immaterial to this discussion. In either case, it is an adaptation to ecological pressures.

The only permanent social unit known to the Basin Shoshoneans was the simple nuclear family. This was a fixed unit. However, functions of production and exploitation were carried on by a much more fluid and complex set of units. Men hunted singly, with other males of the group, and seasonally, with males from other families. Women gathered plant products either alone or in cooperation with other females of the family. All group members acted in concert during the gathering of piñon nuts and when fishing. For large scale rabbit or antelope drives, several families amalgamated into one unit. Productive units were formed by women for weaving blankets and baskets and by men for the manufacture of hard goods. I would suggest that these task performance groups together with associated object clusters and idea frames are cultural units that are formally and functionally distinct from social units. Analogous illustrations from modern family life should readily come to mind.

The foregoing discussion has raised a number of questions. Although it has provided few answers, it has been directed toward the elimination of such statements as: "The fact of the matter is that many of the definitions of culture we cite are only very crudely comparable" (Kroeber and Kluckhohn 1952: 77). Without a notion of systemic structure that integrates cultural categories, there is an arbitrary partitioning of culture which inhibits integration of different forms of cultural data. Without a notion of systemic variation within culture, the organization of cultural data into meaningful units is impossible. And without a notion of cultural units, the search for explanation of cultural organization is futile. Anthropological emphasis has been focused on social units. But other forms of cultural units, because they combine a greater range of cultural things, can tell us much about the operation of the total sociocultural system. Social units combine people into functioning interpersonal groups. But those structural poses that combine social units with implements, ideas, habits, and the like, function to maintain a sociocultural system within an ecological framework.

Archaeological investigations can supplement ethnographic attempts to elucidate processes of cultural-ecological articulation by expanding the range of cultural knowledge both in time and in variety. The ethnographic record is limited and almost daily its scope is diminished by modern industrial expansion. It is, therefore, desirable to establish means for identifying and interpreting differential structural poses in extinct cultural systems. We do not yet know precisely what the relationship may be between long dead cultures and those still living or recently extinct. But, by formulating models for testing our data against a full range of archaeological and ethnological evidence, we will be better able to understand these relationships.

# 3. ARCHAEOLOGICAL SYSTEMATICS

Archaeological interest in artifact assemblages has focused in the past upon the identification of similarities between different collections of excavated materials. Normally this interest has been directed toward the development of means whereby two or more collections may be correlated in time and space to form what are loosely called cultures. In most cases, this has meant simply that a "diagnostic trait" was recognized in each of the collections and this trait was taken to indicate some sort of relationship among the collections. The most obvious weakness of this procedure arises from its concentration of interpretive energies upon one factor only—the "diagnostic trait"—at the expense of other potentially significant artifactual units. The trait may, indeed, be diagnostic but as used in this sense it can yield only correlative information which can do no more than aid in assigning an assemblage to a position with respect to other assemblages in some chronological or comparative scheme. The ignored elements may offer greater possibilities for understanding the technological abilities, economic pursuits, or sociocultural interactions of the people who were the authors of the material objects which constitute an assemblage. Willey and Phillips (1958: 5) have noted the failure of American archaeology to develop satisfactorily at an explanatory level a theoretical structure. Binford (1965: 203-5) has recently suggested that an interpretive framework focused upon selected variations in ideational norms—"diagnostic traits"—may partially account for this failure.

A second difficulty inherent in this approach stems from the vagueness of the proposed relationships which are seldom considered except in spatial or temporal terms. Procedures for the selection of culturally meaningful attributes for defining types in systematically useful ways have not been adequately developed. In the past, attribute identification procedures have been formulated to meet the particular requirements of a specific data set and have been characterized by ad hoc adjustments in the decision-making process when specimen inclusion within a given category was in doubt. Such procedures are subjective and are, therefore, unverifiable by independent investigators. The position taken here is that all conclusions, whether inherently correct or not, based upon intuition-bound notions of culture and loose formulations of interpretive procedure are indefensible because they cannot be independently verified and because they can generate no evaluative mechanisms by means of which preference for one conclusion over another may be demonstrated. These considerations provide strong motivation for a systematization of archaeological methodology.

In a recent paper, Binford (1965) presents an excellent case for a holistic approach to archaeological systematics. He argues for the establishment of multivariate taxonomies as a means for isolating causative factors in the operation of cultural systems and as a basis for identifying regular and predictable relationships among these factors. Binford's discussion is founded upon the general cultural theory formulated by White (1959a; 1959b) in which culture is viewed as a system of adaptive mechanisms with which the member units of human society integrate with their environments. Taylor (1948), Osgood (1951), and Thompson (1958) have also discussed the relationship of archaeological materials to other aspects of culture.

Neither Binford nor White were primarily concerned with developing detailed procedures for constructing a systematic descriptive and classificatory methodology aimed at the establishment of formal-functional taxonomies and the identification of articulations between variables within a cultural system. But Spaulding (1957: 87) has noted that in order to establish "archaeo-sociological" correlations as alternatives to arbitrarily defined taxonomies it is essential that the problem of the classification of archaeological data be satisfactorily treated beforehand. The body of this study is addressed to the formulation of systematic procedures applicable to one category of lithic material.

## SAMPLING

Archaeological methodology may be thought of as a set of procedural devices that serves as a guide in the sampling, description, classification, and explanation of cultural data in an archaeological context.

I will not here take up the discussion of sampling methods except to note that most of the assemblages utilized in this study were not collected in ways that are consistent with the requirements of probability sampling. This fact imposes a number of restrictions upon the handling of data. Vescelius (1960) and Binford (1964) have outlined a number of sampling procedures which may be employed to increase the probability of recovery of representative samples from artifact populations. Freeman and Brown (1964: 126-7) have provided a lucid statement of the rationale underlying such procedures.

## DESCRIPTION

Descriptive methods must serve the needs of the general theory of which they are a part. Spaulding (1960a: 442) has observed that "techniques for recognizing formal attributes logically precede the next problem, that of studying artifact interrelationships in terms of formal attributes . . . the recognized attributes serve as linking constants from artifact to artifact . . . ." Ideally, a descriptive procedure will provide a universally applicable set of defining criteria for each artifact category (e.g. chipped stone) which will specify all the recognized formal attributes of that category. Such a procedure will include a scale of values for each variable attribute against which artifacts can be quantitatively rated on the scales appropriate to the constituent attributes of each artifact. Generally, the formal attributes will be the visible results of the operation upon the artifact of technical and functional processes.

Additionally, and importantly, such a feature representation system for describing artifacts provides for its own expansion when additional formal attributes are recognized. If adequately constructed, it can provide a useful set of data for subsequent analysis of an assemblage. More importantly, it can form a more systematic basis for comparison of different data sets than can impressionistically derived descriptions of artifacts.

Note, however, that Spaulding (1960a: 439-41) has called attention to the existence of qualitative attributes having discreet properties. He has rightly insisted that "any wholesale attempt to replace with measurements the current presence-or-absence observation of [such] attributes would have no utility." It is obvious that not all attributes are amenable to quantification and that excellent interpretive results may be obtained with the use of qualitative data alone (see Deetz 1965 for an example).

I would suggest, however, that each qualitative attribute be examined for quantitative properties. An unresolved example from this study may serve as an illustration. Artifact profiles are given in qualitative terms. Consider, however, that a quantification of profile morphology may provide more significant insights into the processes of flake choice and modification that were operating to produce these profiles. An adequate descriptive procedure will allow quantitative scales to supercede qualitative notation when the value of such replacement can be demonstrated.

## CLASSIFICATION

The classification of archaeological materials is directed toward the discovery of culturally relevant artifactual parameters by means of which extinct cultural units may be identified. Systems of classification should combine descriptive data of a technological and functional nature with data of distribution and association in order to permit the identification of operative cultural units within extinct sociocultural systems. Analysis should be directed toward the identification of quantifiable modality and range of attribute variation and toward the demonstration of covariable constants within the system rather than toward the construction of ideal-type taxonomies based upon superficial resemblances in form.

Brew (1946: 65) and Rouse (1960) have called for a multiplicity of types to "meet new needs." But surely they cannot mean by this that the naming of ever larger numbers of types which "may simply be listed or . . . grouped into culturally meaningful categories" (Rouse 1960: 319) is a useful classificatory procedure. Rather, we need a system that will permit recombinations of attribute isolates into mutually covariate clusters that had operational significance in the cultural system from which they are drawn. Classes so defined are actually hypotheses which state that certain systematic relationships exist between the included variables. As such, they are amenable to testing against different forms of data and are indispensable in the formulation of explanatory inferences from these data.

Spaulding (1960a: 443) has voiced the opinion that a cluster approach to classification exploits "fully the formal information presented by a collection of artifacts." Binford (1962; 1965) has argued that motivation for a multivariate approach is strong. Excellent justification for the adoption of such an approach may be found in results obtained by Struever (1965), Martin and others (1964), and by several authors in Clark and Howell (1966). All of these authors are concerned with the manipulation of artifact types already intuitively defined by others. Sackett (1966: 356-9, 390 fn.) notes that when statistical procedures are employed in typological studies they are, with few exceptions, limited to problems of assigning formally intermediate specimens to impressionistically defined classes.

In this study, I am concerned with the problem of recognizing artifact classes on the basis of definable attribute covariation. I begin with the assumption that artifact types are real and that they may be discovered through a process that recognizes constituent structure in attribute clustering. I begin with attributes and work toward artifacts. This procedure is diametrically opposite to that proposed by Rouse (1939) and implicitly followed by most archaeologists. But if the foregoing discussion has any validity, the approach followed here should lead ultimately to a deeper understanding of the cultural nature of archaeological data.

# 4. PROCEDURES

Motivation for this study lies in a desire to further the utilization of total archaeological resources in the broadening search for understanding of cultural processes. Specifically, it is directed toward the expansion of the scope of lithic analysis through the presentation of certain descriptive and classificatory devices. These methods are applied to lithic assemblages from a number of Paleo-Indian sites. The results obtained suggest that a more complete understanding of the Paleo-Indian Stage may be gained by application, to the whole range of data pertaining to it, of more rigorous procedures than were employed in the past (Wilmsen 1968).

The data for this study were derived from eight Paleo-Indian sites: Blackwater, Horner, Levi, Lindenmeier, Quad, Shoop, Vernon, and Williamson. A total of 2,139 artifacts was selected from the collections for intensive examination. Data from one other site, Elida, were obtained but not used because the amount of pertinent material was insufficient to be statistically significant.

## SITE SELECTION

A number of considerations guided the selection of sites. Primary among these was a desire to incorporate into the analysis as representative a geographical range as practicable. A determined effort was made, therefore, to utilize collections from sites in all parts of the known Paleo-Indian range. An examination of the distribution map (Fig. 1) will reveal that this effort has been reasonably successful. The northeastern part of this range is the only under-represented area containing major sites.

A second important consideration was that the sites chosen should represent a wide range within the known Paleo-Indian time span. That this condition has also been met may be seen by reference to Table 1.

The third consideration guiding site selection was collection size. Only large collections and those that are comprehensive in their representation of the artifact variation in the sites from which they are drawn are useful to a study of the kind presented here. Table 2 lists the total assemblage size and total sample size for each site.

In addition to the data from the Paleo-Indian collections, data were obtained from two other assemblages. These serve as intertraditional controls over the Paleo-Indian data. Control samples were drawn from the Denbigh component at Cape Krusenstern and a Woodland sample (Big Kiokee Creek) from Georgia. The first of these was chosen because it has been suggested that there are close relationships between Denbigh and Paleo-Indian materials (Giddings 1951; Witthoft 1952: 489-92). The latter was chosen because it represents a demonstrably later occupation in an area that has produced Paleo-Indian materials and it should, therefore, provide a test for differences and similarities between the various collections from those areas.

## SAMPLE SELECTION

The initial step in working with each collection was the selection of a representative sample from the body of available artifacts. In each of four collections, the total assemblage size was small enough so that the entire collection could be used. The remaining collections were so large, however, that use of the entire collections was precluded. There simply was not enough time to examine each artifact; therefore, an attempt was made to draw a representative sample from each of these collections.

Although individual site conditions dictated modifications, sample selection procedures for each of these collections were structured in a generally similar way:
1. The entire collection was laid out.
2. All non-lithic material and non-chipped material (e.g. abrading stones, hammer stones) as well as all chipped bifaces and cores were segregated, counted, and recorded. These specimens were not used in the analysis. The quantity of this material was generally very small.
3. The remainder of the collection was divided into:
   a. Unutilized raw flakes;
   b. Unmodified but utilized flakes;
   c. Tools—characterized by retouch modification:
      1) Whole;
      2) Fragments.

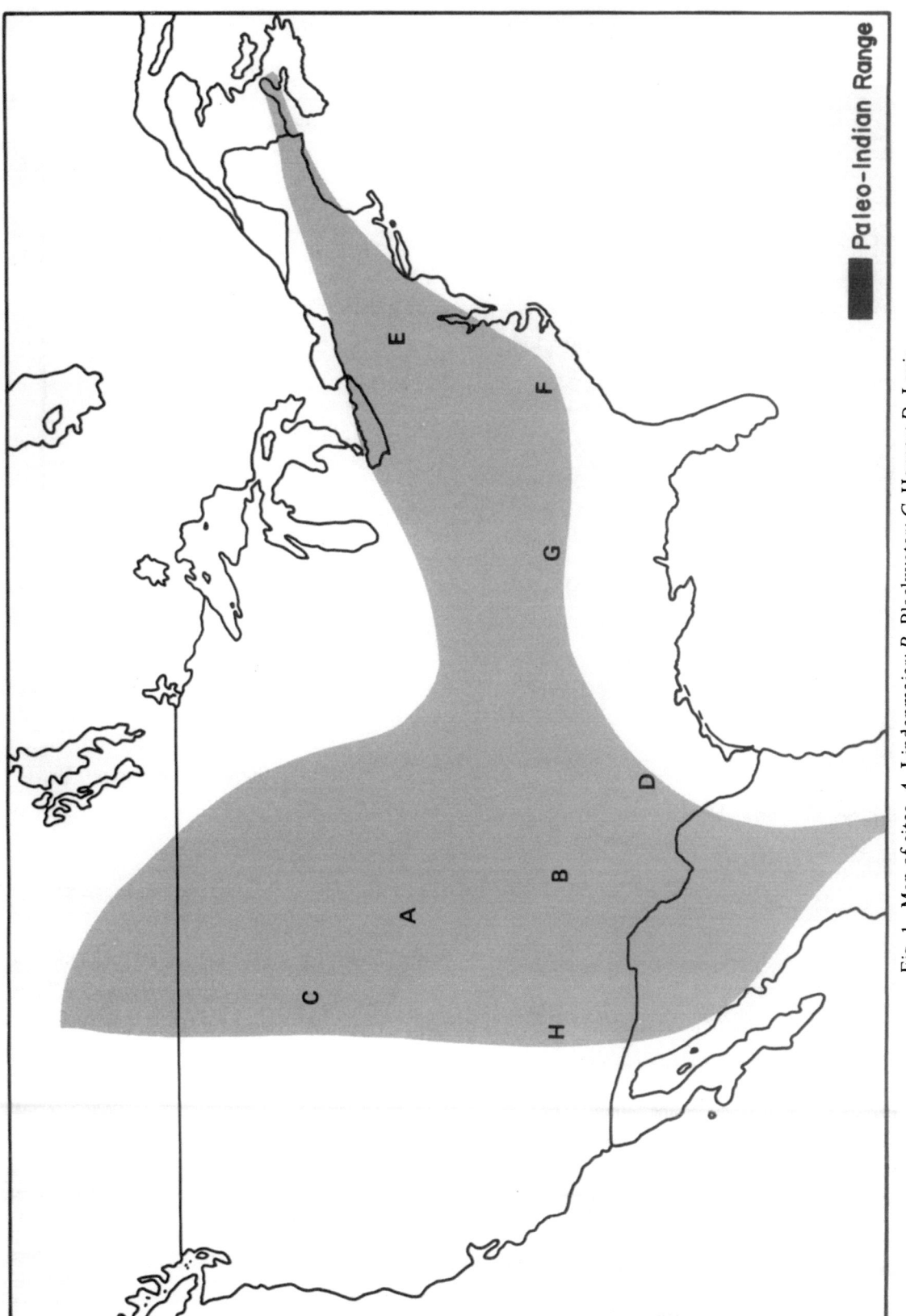

Fig. 1. Map of sites. *A*, Lindenmeier; *B*, Blackwater; *C*, Horner; *D*, Levi; *E*, Shoop; *F*, Williamson; *G*, Quad; *H*, Vernon.

## TABLE 1
### Chronology of Sites

| Radiocarbon Age Determination* | Estimated Time Placement |
|---|---|
| Horner (6876 ± 250) — ? 6750 ± 150 | ↑ ? |
| Levi ———————— ? 7350 ± 150 | |
| ————— ? 9300 ± 160 | ↑ ? Vernon ↓ ? |
| | Shoop — Williamson — Quad |
| Lindenmeier (10780 ± 135) | |
| Blackwater (11170 ± 360) | |

*Probably valid dates in parentheses.

4. All categories were further divided according to the following criteria:
   a. Type of raw material;
   b. Gross size differences;
   c. Presence or absence of striking platform;
   d. Position of retouch.
5. A total sample size was decided upon; a proportional number of specimens was drawn from each artifact set resulting from steps 3 and 4. Unmodified, unutilized flakes without striking platforms and chips less than 15 mm. in gross length were, in general, not selected.
6. Each selected specimen was subjected to the analytical procedures described below. The data obtained were entered on IBM Porta-Punch cards for subsequent processing. The standard code sheets used to control data recording are reproduced in Figure 2.

## DEFINITION OF VARIABLES

Each artifact was described in standard terms. Sackett (1966: 360) has cogently remarked that

a major problem in designing an attributal framework for such intergrading artifacts as stone tools is to determine the proper breadth or scope of its component systems ... no attribute system attempts to provide an exhaustive inventory of the variables relevant to its artifact group, and no doubt a mixture of technological, functional, and stylistic elements are reflected in each of them.

## TABLE 2
### Assemblage and Sample Sizes

| Site | Total Assemblage Size | Total Sample Size |
|---|---|---|
| Lindenmeier | 7,000 (estimate) | 747 |
| Blackwater | Approximately 224 (Clovis level) in all collections – of these about 175 have good provenience data | 118 |
| Horner | 210 tools<br>400 (estimate) flakes, chips, scraps | 120 |
| Levi | 442 tools<br>several thousand chips and scraps | 139 |
| Shoop | 800 | 181 |
| Williamson | 1,500 (estimate) | 191 |
| Quad | 1,000 (estimate) | 444 |
| Vernon | 2,334 plus a large number of specimens from the surface and an unknown number in private collections | 199 |
| | Total | 2,139 |

A strong effort has been made in this study to recognize these intergrading propensities of stone artifacts and to design a descriptive and classificatory system that will take these propensities into account. This effort has not been entirely successful. One instance in which it failed has already been cited. However, a number of scaling devices are introduced which suggest that further efforts in this direction will be worthwhile.

Furthermore, an attempt was made to distinguish those elements of formal variation that stem from technological processes of artifact manufacture from those elements that are the product of artifact utilization. The identification of wear patterns was carried out macroscopically in most cases and, therefore, is only grossly indicative of utilization variation. These gross patterns are, nonetheless, instructive. Stylistic variation in non-projectile specimens was not recognized and was not systematically sought. While such variation may be present in the collections, it is not readily apparent.

A total of 42 variables was used in this study. This total hardly represents an exhaustive attribute list which might pertain to the materials studied. Nor does it include all of the variables recognized in the collections. Several artifact categories, such as cores, with their attendant distinguishing attribute sets, are not included because of their absence or near absence from most of the collections. It should also be noted that the two collections (Blackwater and Elida) examined first were the smallest, and in many ways the most unsatisfactory, of all those studied. Because of this, the attribute set design was not completed until the next collections became available. Data were also not obtained for all variables in the Shoop sample. Data from these sites are, therefore, much less complete than they are for the remaining sites. Indeed, as was noted above, data from the Elida sample was not incorporated into the analysis at all.

The variables are summarized below. The format of presentation of the variables follows the order of data notation on the code sheets.

For obvious reasons, unutilized flakes are represented by Card I only (Fig. 2a). All tools and most utilized flakes are represented by both Card I and Card II (Fig. 2b). The first data set entered on Card I is an identification set which designates the site and specimen number of the artifact represented by that card. This information is repeated on Card II when this card is needed. The card number (I or II) is also

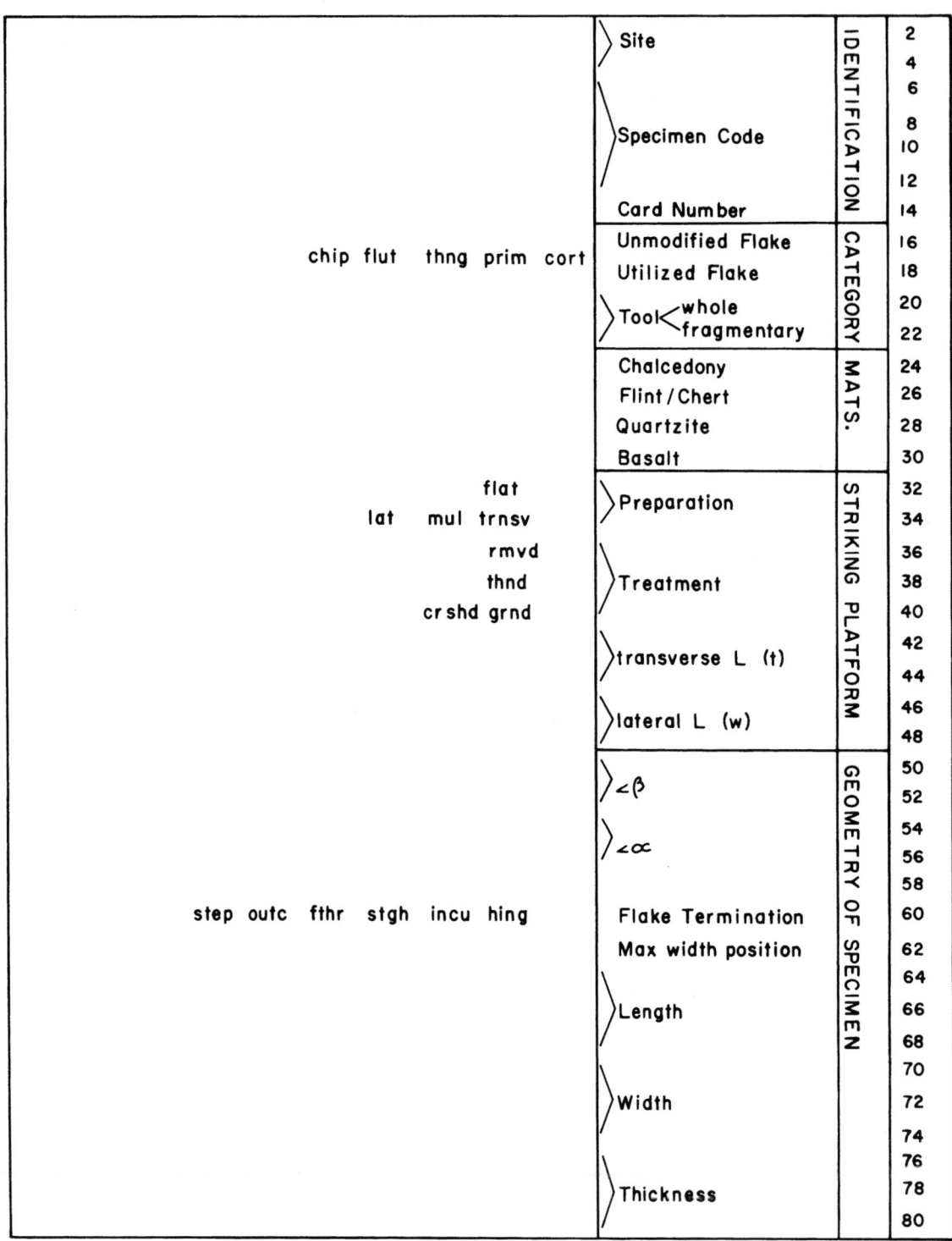

Fig. 2a. Code key for data recording — code sheet for Card I.

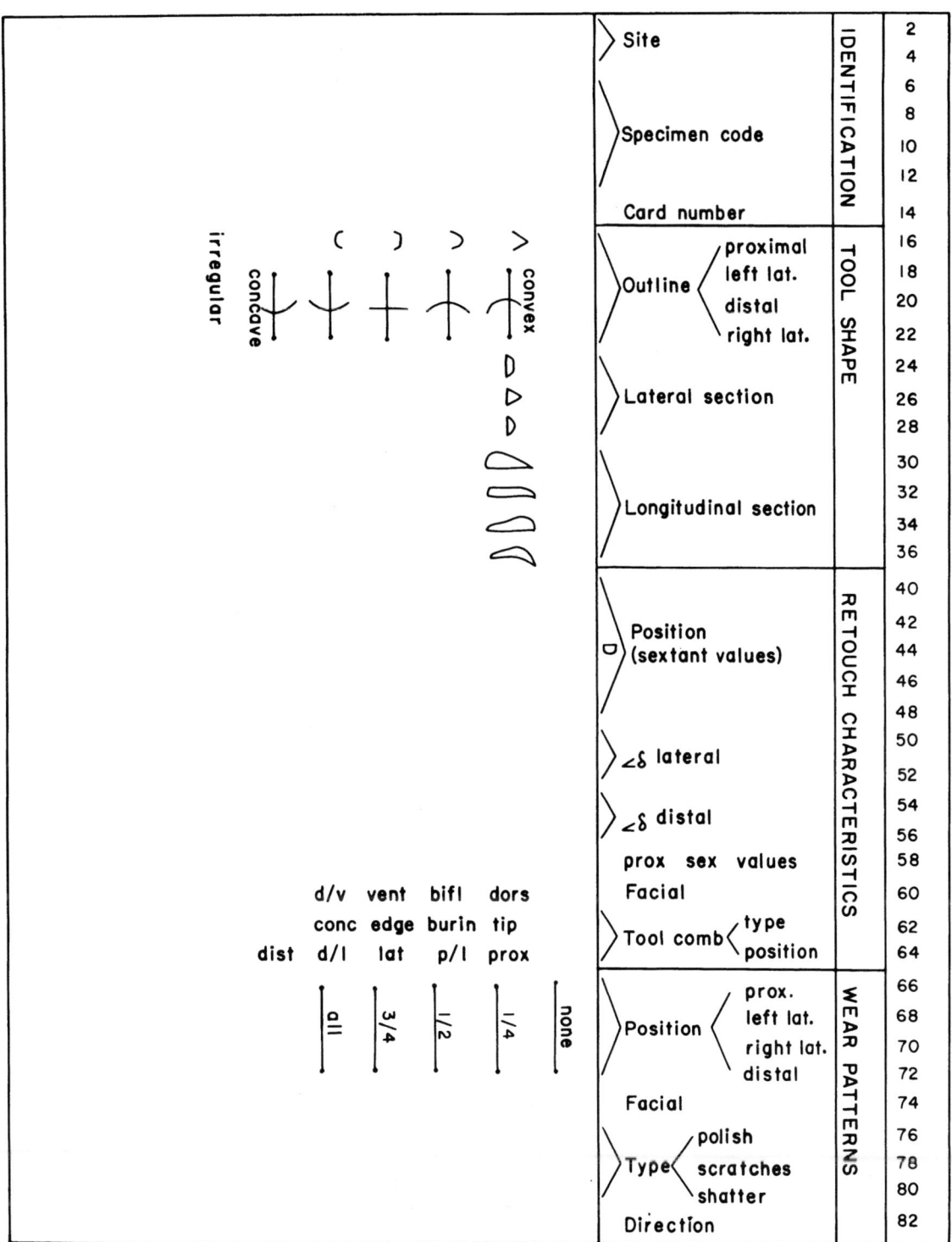

Fig. 2b. Code key for data recording – code sheet for Card II.

noted. In a number of the collections examined, specimen numbers are assigned only to projectile points and a few other "attractive" forms. Serial numeration of specimens was adopted for these collections.

*Category.* This class includes four variables:
1. Unmodified, unutilized flakes—flakes, either whole or fragmentary, that exhibit no macroscopic evidence of retouch or use after removal from a core;
2. Utilized flakes—flakes which exhibit evidence of use but not of retouch;
3. Tools, whole—flakes which have been modified by retouch on one or more edges;
4. Tools, fragmentary—these are broken specimens of 3, above.

*Materials.* An attempt was made to distinguish between the various raw material types present in the collections. However, the various forms of quartzitic rocks from which the vast majority of the artifacts are made intergrade to a considerable degree. It was, therefore, possible to make only gross distinctions between these types. Non-quartzitic raw materials are extremely rare in the collections and have been grouped under the heading Basalt.

*Striking Platform Characteristics.* This class includes five variables:
1. Preparation—prior to detachment of a flake, the platform area is preconditioned to receive the detaching blow by the removal of one or more chips. These chips leave visible scars and it is these scars that are documented here (Fig. 3).
2. Treatment—notation of post-detachment removal or thinning of the platform.
3. Abrasion—notation of the presence of evidence of grinding, rubbing, or crushing of the platform (Fig. 4).
4. Tranverse length (t)—the dorso-ventral dimension of the platform taken at the point of percussion or pressure (Fig. 3).
5. Lateral length (w)—maximum lateral dimension of the platform (Fig. 3). Punch-card space restrictions were such that only two columns could be devoted to this variable; therefore, the largest dimension recorded was 9.9 mm. All dimensions greater than this value were recorded as 9.9 mm. The Levi sample was the only one in which this procedure skewed the data to any extent.

*Geometry of Specimen.* This class contains six variables:

1. Angle *beta*—the angle formed between the plane of the striking platform and the plane of the ventral surface of the flake. Chandler (1929), Paterson (1937), and Barnes (1939) have considered a similar measurement (see also Ascher and Ascher 1965). I measured this angle with a polar coordinate grid and lens stand (Fig. 5). In a few cases, a jewler's comparator was used.
2. Angle *alpha*—the angle formed between the axis of percussion (a line drawn perpendicularly to the striking platform at the point of percussion) and the medial axis of the flake (Fig. 6). A radial grid was used for this measurement. Readings are to the nearest two degrees.
3. Maximum width position—notation of the point of maximum lateral dimension along a seven-step scale (Fig. 7).
4. Length—the dimension measured on the medial axis of the flake (Fig. 7).
5. Width—the maximum dimension taken perpendicularly to length (Fig. 7).
6. Thickness—maximum transverse dimension taken below the bulb of percussion (Fig. 7).

*Tool Shape Characteristics.* This class includes six variables:
1. Outline—each edge was treated as an independent variable; therefore, there are four outline variables. Each edge was rated on a scale of curvature from strongly convex, through straight, to deeply concave. In addition, the scales for proximal and distal edges include 0 values which were assigned in those instances in which these edges converge to a point.
2. Lateral section—section profiles were visually determined.
3. Longitudinal section—section profiles were visually determined.

*Retouch Characteristics.* This class includes eleven variables.
1. Position—the location of edge retouch. Determined by placing the specimen on a polar coordinate grid upon which an axis centered upon a six part division of the circle is drawn. Each artifact was centered on the grid with its medial axis overlying the grid axis; the number of degrees of arc (to the nearest $10°$) subtended by retouch was recorded for each sextant (Fig. 8).
2. Angle *delta* lateral—the angle between the ventral and dorsal surfaces of an artifact at those lateral positions where either retouch or use scars are present (Fig. 9).

3. Angle *delta* distal—the angle between the ventral and dorsal surfaces of an artifact at those distal positions where either retouch or use scars are present (Fig. 10). Measurements for angles *delta* are to the nearest 5°.
4. Facial—a notation that indicates the surface on which retouch scars occur.
5. Tool combinations—the first entry indicates the type of appended tool form; the second entry locates it.

*Wear Patterns.* These nine variables were, with few exceptions, macroscopically examined and are, therefore, inconsistently and inadequately noted. They are not intended to form a major part of this study. But they are recorded because they do point to interesting avenues for further research.

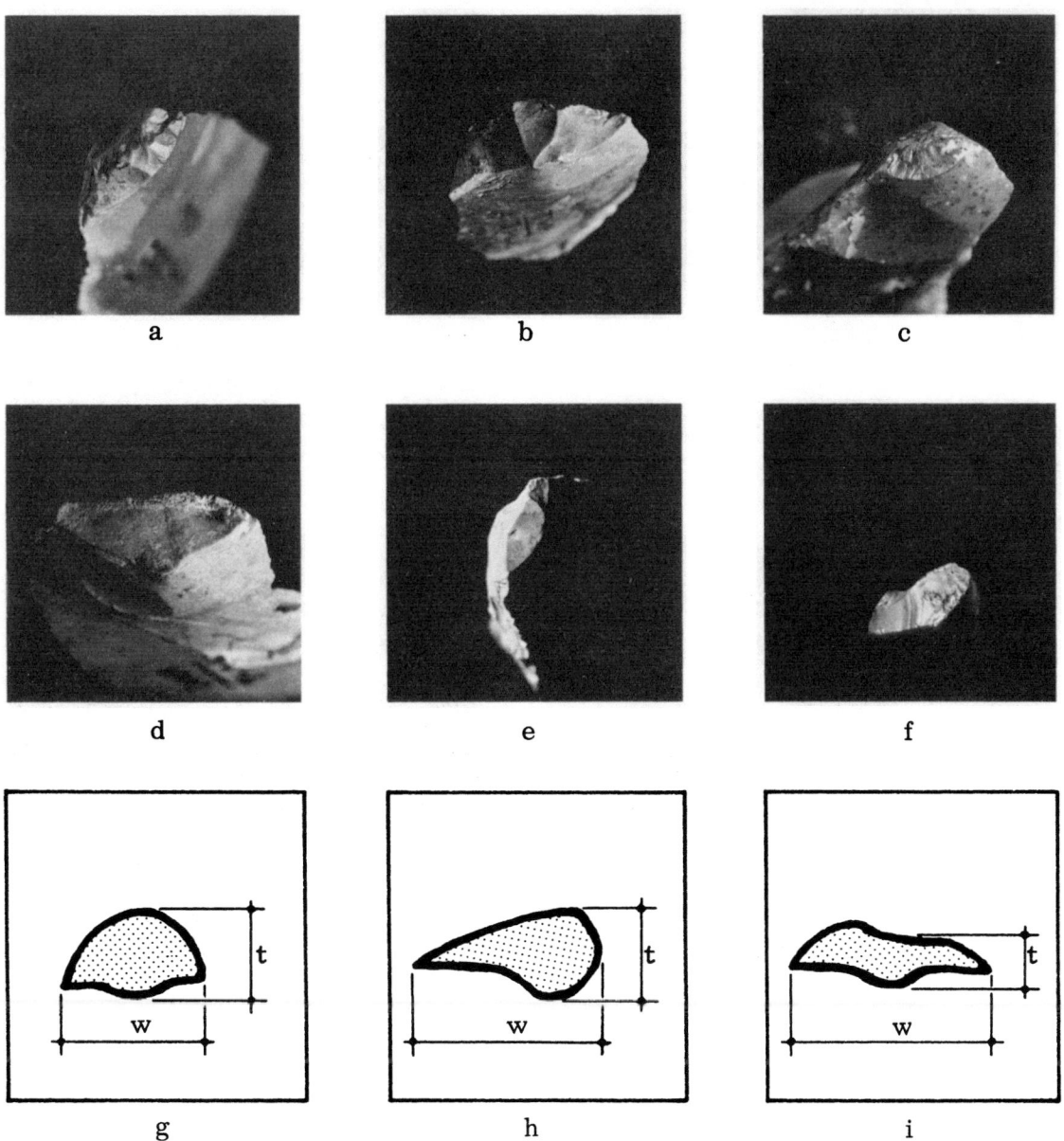

Fig. 3. Platform preparation and dimensions. *a*, transverse, t = 3.5 mm., Lindenmeier; *b*, transverse, t = 11 mm., Levi; *c*, multiple, t = 4.7 mm., Lindenmeier; *d*, flat, t = 10 mm., Levi; *e*, flat, t = 3.5 mm., Shoop; *f*, lateral, t = 6 mm., Lindenmeier; *g - i*, platform measurements.

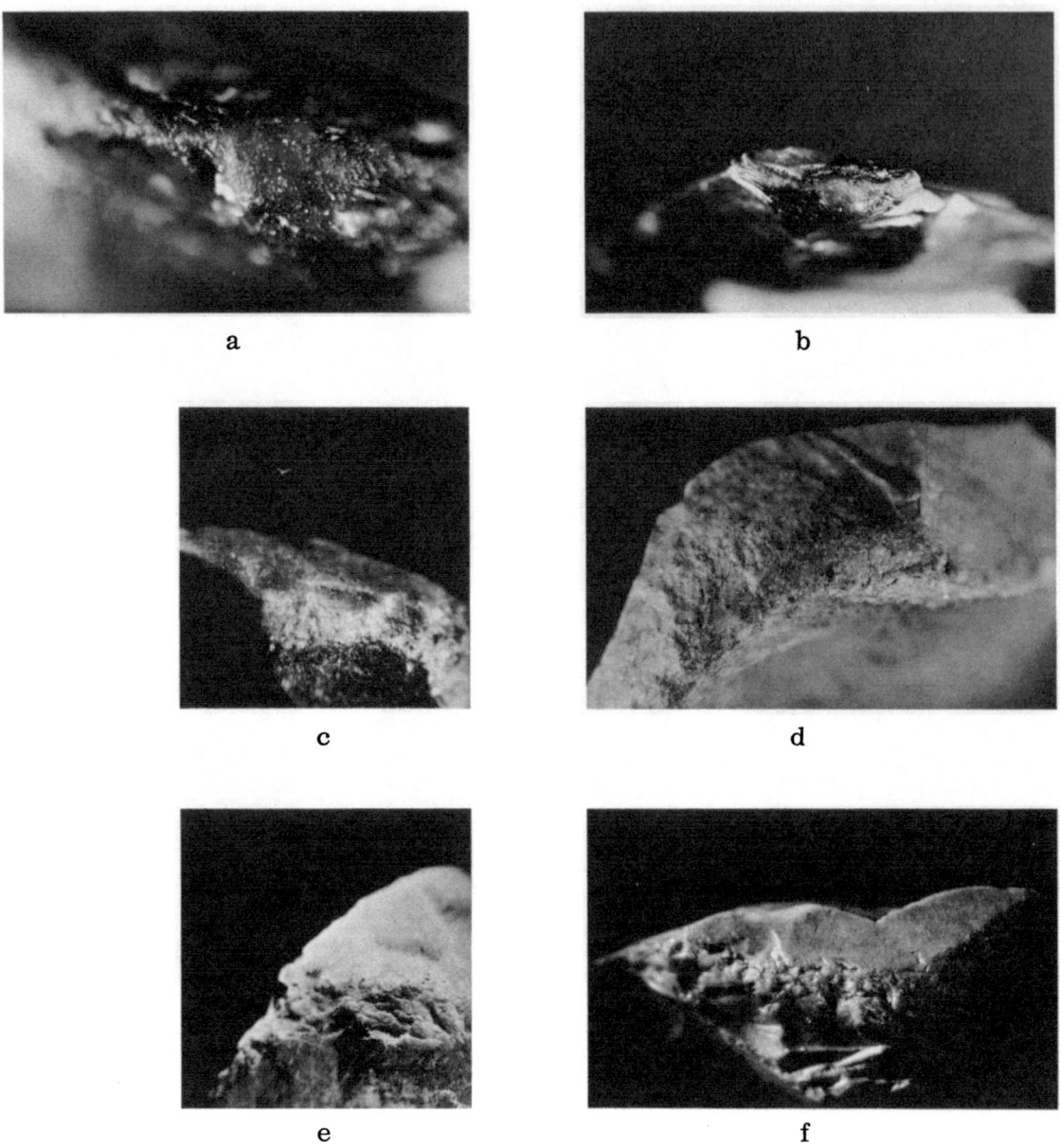

Fig. 4. Platform abrasion. *a*, abrasion over full platform surface, Lindenmeier; *b*, abrasion on dorsal edge only, Blackwater; *c*, abraded dorsal edge, Williamson; *d*, abrasion on quartzite specimen, Lindenmeier; *e*, dorsal edge crushing, Lindenmeier; *f*, flat platform with crushed dorsal edge, Shoop. (*a*, three times actual size; *c* - *e*, two times actual size.)

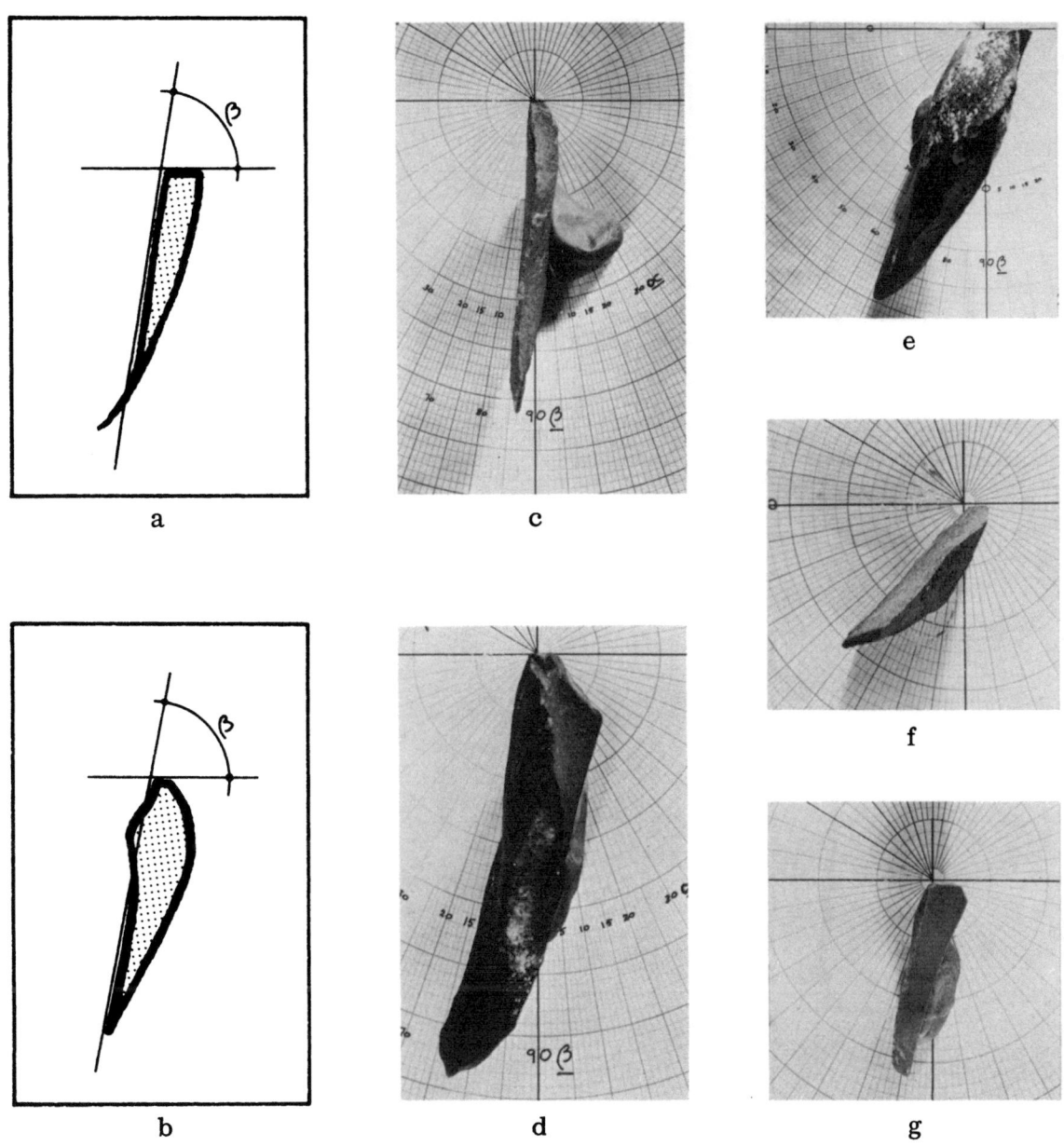

Fig. 5. Flake angle ($< \beta$) measurements. *a - b*, method of measuring flake angle; *c*, $\beta = 85°$; *d*, $\beta = 80°$; *e*, $\beta = 65°$; *f*, $\beta = 48°$; *g*, $\beta = 72°$.

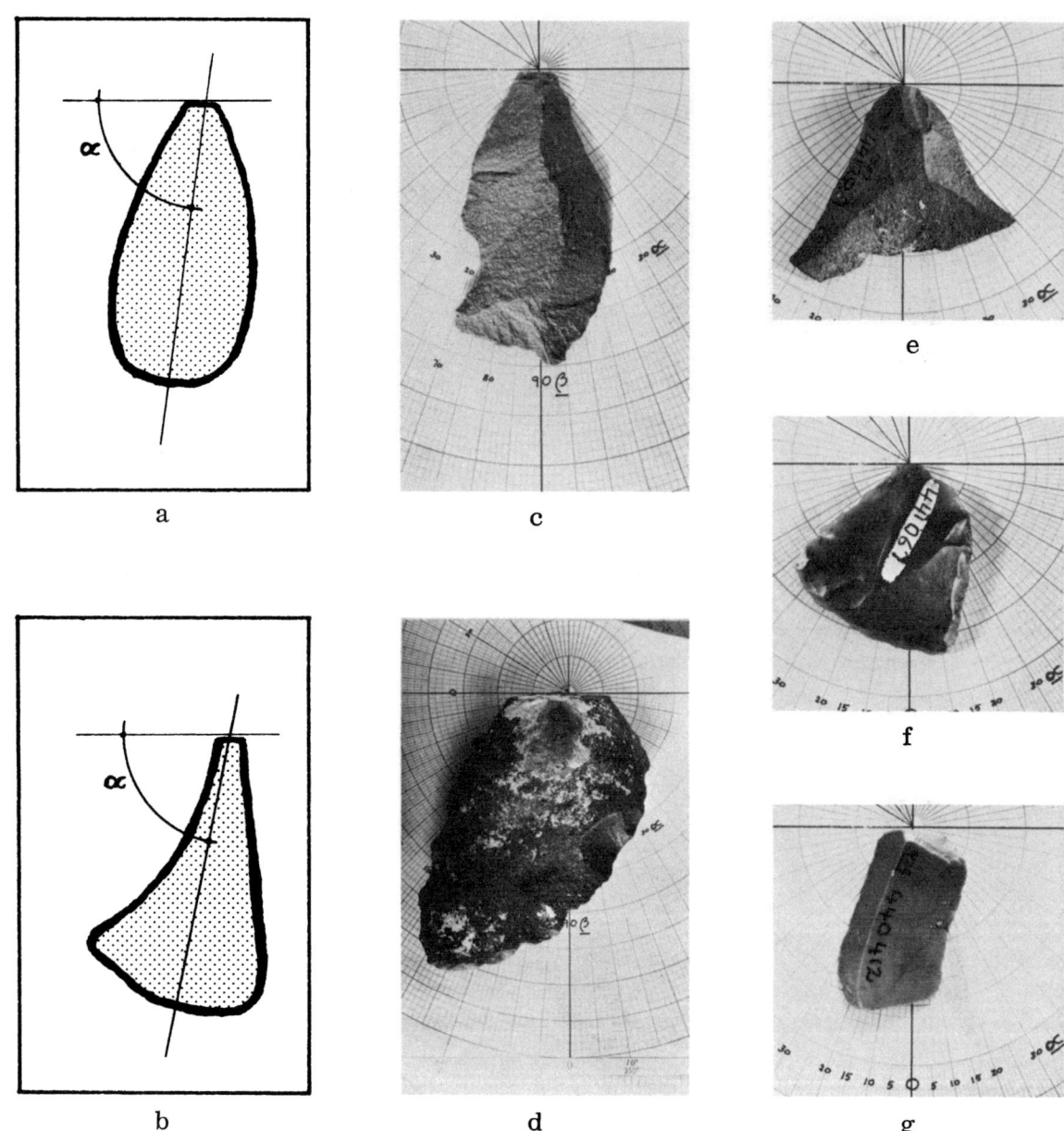

Fig. 6. Medial axis ($< \alpha$) measurements. $a$ - $b$, method of measuring medial axis; $c$, $\alpha = 0°$; $d$, $\alpha = 15°$; $e$, $\alpha = 3°$; $f$, $\alpha = 7°$; $g$, $\alpha = 5°$.

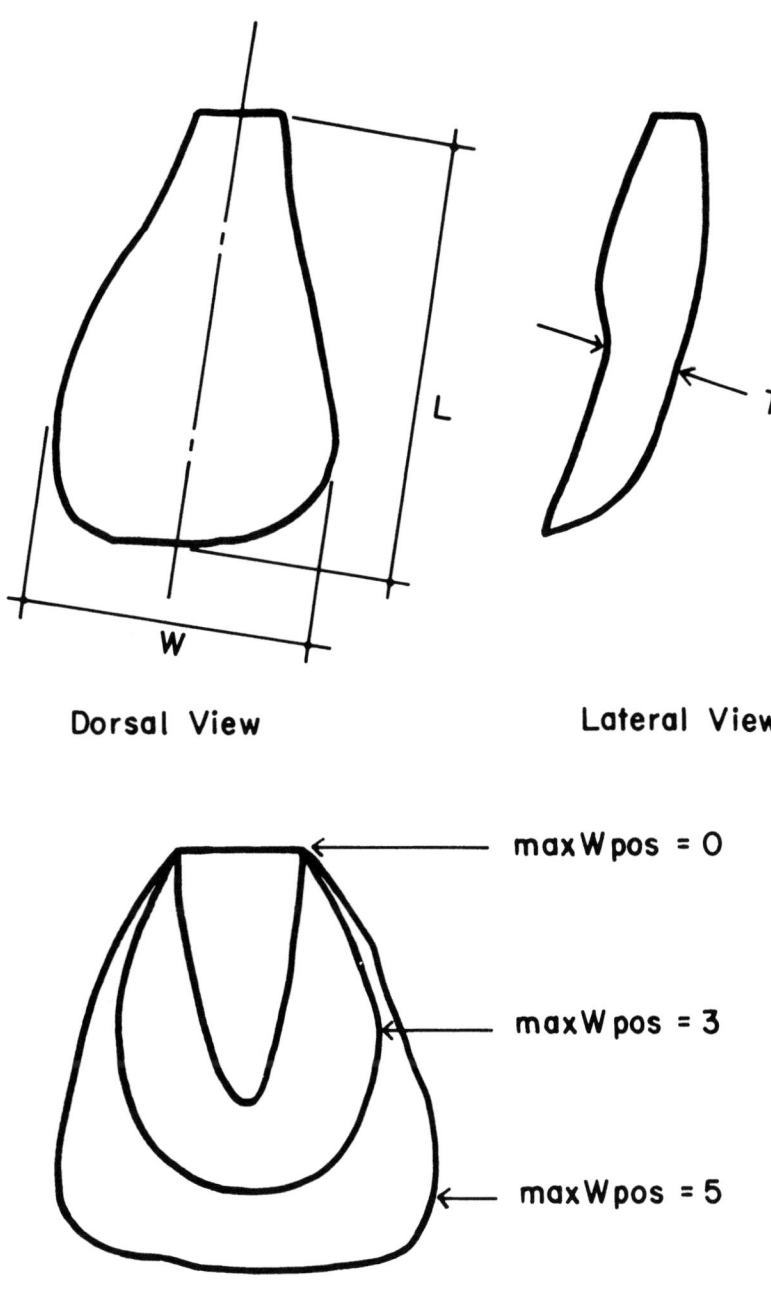

Fig. 7. Flake dimensions. Maximum width position = maxWpos.

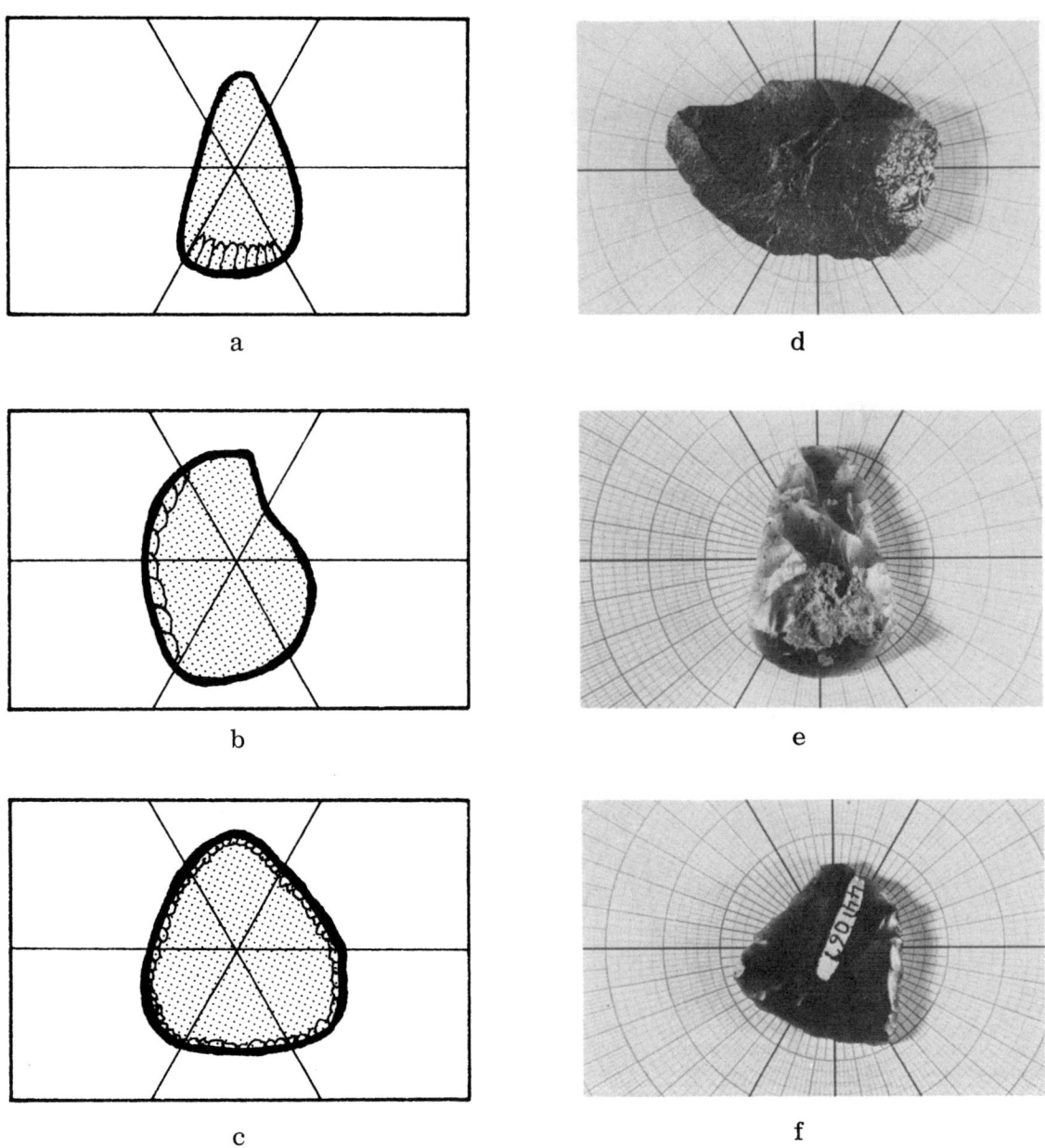

Fig. 8. Notation for retouch position. *a*, distal retouch only: values, 0-00600; *b*, lateral retouch only: values, 0-66000; *c*, retouch on all edges: values, 6-66666; *d*, specimen retouch values, 0-16052; *e*, specimen retouch values, 6-66666; *f*, specimen retouch values, 2-66666.

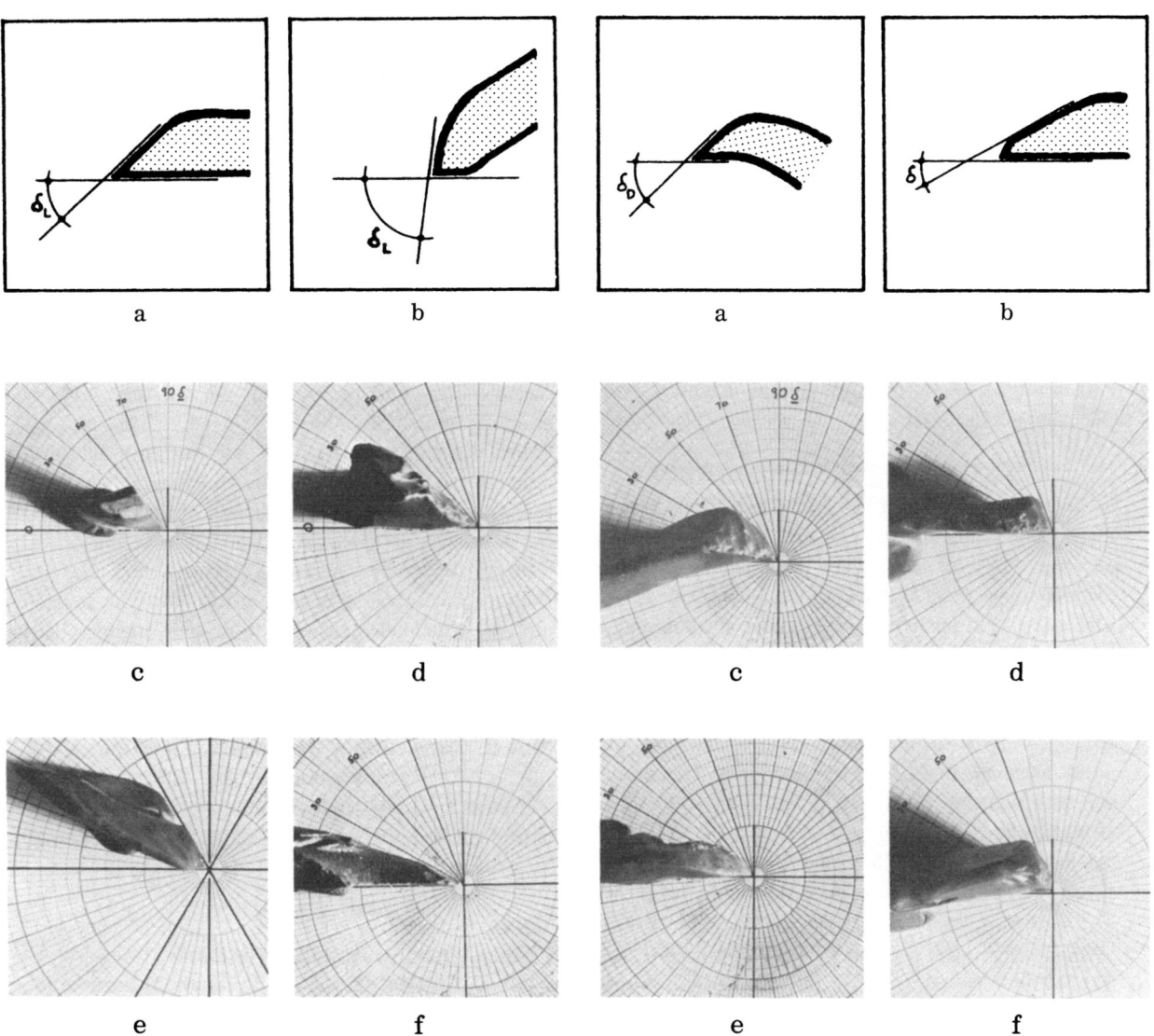

Fig. 9. Lateral edge ($< \delta_L$) measurement. *a*, measurement of edge with flat ventral surface; *b*, measurement of edge with ventral retouch; *c*, $\delta_L = 50°$; *d*, $\delta_L = 50°$; *e*, $\delta_L = 60°$; *f*, $\delta_L = 30°$.

Fig. 10. Distal edge ($< \delta_D$) measurement. *a*, measurement of edge with curved ventral surface; *b*, measurement of edge with slight use damage; *c*, $\delta_D = 65°$; *d*, $\delta_D = 70°$; *e*, $\delta_D = 50°$; *f*, $\delta_D = 90°$.

# 5. THE DATA

## SOURCES OF DATA

The following discussion will summarize the descriptive and interpretive literature pertaining to each of the sites considered in this study. It will include information about the present locations of the collections and will acknowledge the assistance given me by those who now control the collections. Procedures used to structure sample selection from each site are discussed.

## Blackwater (Number One Locality)

This site, has come to be called the Clovis Site or Blackwater Number One Locality (Fig. 1, B). It lies on the edge of Blackwater Draw in the Llano Estacado near the town of Portales, New Mexico. The site contains a number of superimposed components that span the entire Paleo-Indian period and extend into the Archaic. The lowermost component has yielded 224 artifacts, including Clovis points, which are attributable to the Clovis Horizon. Side tools are most abundant while endscrapers are rare. Remains of mammoth occur in direct association with these artifacts. A radiocarbon age of 11,170 ± 360 years has been assigned to this component (Haynes 1964: 1408). This study is concerned only with the Clovis Horizon at this site. (Primary sources are: Howard 1935; Cotter 1938; Sellards 1952; Warnica 1966; and Haynes and Agogino 1960.) Hester (MS) documents the inadequacy of most of the archaeological work at the site and notes that the original provenience of many of the artifacts is in doubt. For this reason, only those artifacts recovered by the El Llano Archaeological Society in 1962-63 under the direction of James M. Warnica and a very few specimens from the collection of the Paleo-Indian Institute have been included in this study. The El Llano Society kept all specimens that were found and accurately recorded the positions of these specimens. Gratitude is expressed to James M. Warnica and to George A. Agogino for making this material available to me.

## Quad

The Quad Site is located on the banks of a creek tributary to the Tennessee River near Decatur in northern Alabama (Fig. 1, G). It is essentially a surface site although a minor excavation has indicated that some geological and archaeological stratigraphic variation occurs (Cambron and Hulse 1960). Paleo-Indian and Archaic materials are mixed on the surface. A great variety of fluted and non-fluted points are present but forms of the Dalton type predominate. Stemmed and notched points are abundantly present in a variety of forms. Many other flaked tool types are present in quantity but no grinding tools have been reported. There are no faunal associations. Artifacts are concentrated in a number of discrete locations on slightly elevated ridges. A 50 per cent sample was drawn and structured to include specimens from all these locations. The primary source is Soday (1954). Dr. Soday, of Tulsa, Oklahoma, is a perceptive amateur archaeologist who collects in a thorough manner. His collection includes flakes, chips, and fragmentary tools as well as exhibit specimens and is accurately catalogued, but whether or not the assemblage is truly representative of the artifact population of the site cannot be determined. Dr. Soday went to considerable effort and personal expense to send his entire collection to me for examination. His generosity shall not be forgotten.

## Shoop

The Shoop Site is situated on a series of low knolls atop an irregular plateau bordering the Susquehanna Valley in east central Pennsylvania (Fig. 1, E). Total extent of the site exceeds twenty acres. All of the artifacts from the site were collected on the present surface but many of these were brought to this surface by plowing. The site has yielded fluted points, scrapers, gravers, and other tool forms. Endscraper forms predominate. A number of small triangular points as well as a few stemmed points are in the collections. There are no ground or pecked tools. No faunal associations have been observed. Witthoft (1952) has presented the only extensive discussion of the site. His work has depended heavily upon that of several amateurs among whom Soday is prominent. The sample used in this study was drawn from Soday's collection and from the Gordon collection in the U.S. National Museum. Every artifact in these collections that met the conditions for inclusion in this study was used. Soday's collection is inclusive, as is his Quad collection, but Gordon was highly selective in his collecting.

## Williamson

The Williamson Site is situated on a long, low ridge in the Piedmont section of Virginia (Fig. 1, F). Thousands of flakes and cores were once present for a distance of approximately one mile along this ridge but extensive relic hunting and lapidary collecting have made artifacts rare. The site is entirely on the surface; a trench cut through the area in 1965 failed to expose any artifact bearing strata. The site contains fluted points, many of which are unfinished, and a great number of endscrapers. Other tool types are present in proportionately few numbers. Archaic implements are scattered on the periphery of the site. No faunal associations exist. The only publication on the site is that by McCary (1951) who also owns the major collection from the site. Dr. McCary was most gracious in making his collection available, in providing a place for me to work, and in giving me a substantial amount of his time. A sample of about 15 per cent of the total available collection (approximately 1,500 specimens) was drawn for inclusion in this study. Because of its large size and because McCary was the first to collect on the site, this assemblage is probably reasonably representative of the site artifact population.

## Lindenmeier

This site, perhaps the most important of all Paleo-Indian sites, is in Colorado near the Wyoming state line (Fig. 1, A). It is situated on a terrace bench at the edge of the Rocky Mountain foothills and overlooks the High Plains. The site has been productive over an area more than one-half mile long and one-eighth mile wide. Within this area, a number of artifact concentrations occur, some of which are more than 10,000 square feet in extent. The site is stratified and contains extinct bison remains in association with Folsom cultural material. Remains of deer and rabbit are also present in quantity as are those of antelope. The lower levels are assignable to the Folsom Complex while the upper levels are attributable to later Paleo-Indian and Archaic occupations. The sample for this study was drawn only from artifacts found in the Folsom levels and great care was taken to segregate other materials from these. A 10 per cent sample (approximately) of the 7,000 artifacts in the Folsom collection was utilized. Roberts kept all tools and at least half of the debitage uncovered in excavation. We may reasonably assume that the assemblage is statistically representative. The site is rich in a great variety of tool types and a concerted effort was made to include representative samples of all types from all portions of the site. Publications on the site have been inadequate. (Principal sources are: Roberts 1935, 1936; Bryan and Ray 1940; and a summary in Wormington 1957.) The major collection is in the U.S. National Museum. My debt to the Smithsonian Institution and its staff in the Office of Anthropology is recorded in the preface to this monograph. In addition, I must note my gratitude to Marie Wormington who gave large portions of her time in order to make available to me that part of the Lindenmeier assemblage in her care in the Denver Museum of Natural History.

## Vernon

The Vernon Site is situated on top of a flat erosional bench in east central Arizona (Fig. 1, H). Artifacts occur only on the surface and exploratory excavations have revealed a thin soil mantle over bedrock that precludes stratigraphy of any sort. The site was systematically collected by members of the Chicago Natural History (now Field) Museum Southwest Expedition. A grid was established and randomly structured for artifact retrieval. Because this systematic approach was followed, the presence of two components was detected. One of these was concentrated in the northern sector of the site and consists mainly of flaked tools including fluted points. The other component, which occured primarily in the southern third of the site, includes several cobble tools and two manos. A sample from the southern sector was drawn for this study; approximately 10 per cent of the 2,334 artifacts from the excavated samples was utilized. There is no publication on the site but a paper describing the collection was read at the 1963 meeting of the Society for American Archaeology (Longacre 1963). I wish to thank Paul Martin of the Field Museum for his generosity in making the collection available to me. I am also grateful to John Fritz for assisting me in my work on this collection.

## Levi

The Levi Rockshelter is located in the canyon of a small tributary of the Pedernales River in the Hill

Country of central Texas (Fig. 1, D). It is a deeply stratified site with a long Paleo-Indian sequence. The sample for this study was drawn from Zone IV which yielded half—422 specimens—of the tools recovered from the site. This zone is characterized by Angostura-Plain view points, side-scrapers, blades, and polyhedral cores, as well as a large number of burins and burin spalls. Grinding stones are present. Faunal associations are primarily rodents, rabbits, and small carnivores (including an extinct raccoon). Bison, antelope, and white-tailed deer are also represented. Snail and mussel shells are common as are hackberry seeds. Radiocarbon analysis of three shell samples has yielded inconsistent results. These samples yielded ages ranging from 9,300 to 6,700 years ago. All of the tools from Zone IV which met the requirements of this study were utilized as were about 1 per cent of the 5,000 chips recovered from this zone. Alexander (1963) has published the only extensive reference on the site. I am grateful to him for giving me access to the collection which is currently housed in the Department of Anthropology, Bryn Mawr College.

### Horner

The Horner Site is situated on a terrace overlooking Sage Creek near Cody, Wyoming (Fig. 1, C). This shallow site has yielded the remains of some 180 bison together with 210 tools, including Eden and Scottsbluff points. There are, in addition, some 400 chips and utilized flakes. All of the applicable tools and 10 per cent of the chips and flakes were examined for this study. Two radiocarbon age determinations are available for the site—$6876 \pm 250$ years and $6920 \pm 500$ years (Wormington 1957: 128). Except for brief notices (Jepsen 1951, 1953), there are no publications on the site. My thanks are due to Waldo Wedel and Glen L. Jepsen for allowing me to use their unpublished material and for granting me the privilege of examining the collection which is presently in the U.S. National Museum.

### Denbigh

This collection was made from a series of well-defined beach ridges on Cape Krusenstern on the Bering Strait. Independent radiocarbon dating of this complex at the Onion Portage Site has indicated an age of 4,500 years for Denbigh. Although Giddings and Witthoft once saw Paleo-Indian antecedents in Denbigh, it is now more reasonably seen as an expression of a seasonal adaptation to Arctic hunting conditions along the coast and inland (see Taylor 1966 for a lucid statement of this view). I was fortunately able to work with the Denbigh material in Giddings' laboratory in 1964. He and Mrs. Giddings were most gracious to me at that time.

### Big Kiokee Creek

This collection was purchased for $500 by the U. S. National Museum in 1901. It was obtained from a Dr. Roland Steiner who had gathered the material from what is called a large Indian soapstone quarry and village site. The collection includes 18,718 specimens among which are points, scrapers, rubbing stones, polished and grooved axes, mortars and pestles, stone beads, carved stone pipes, and some pottery. These materials may represent a number of successive occupations. They probably belong to the time period of about A.D. 1000. All specimens suitable for this study that could be found were used; there were only 59 of these.

## DESCRIPTION OF THE DATA

The variables are treated as grouped data by site. Each variable is first considered individually and then in combination with other variables. The concept of grouping is not new in archaeology. Artifacts are commonly treated as members of a class. Childe (1923) insisted that unique specimens (that is, those not members of a class) are not cultural; he therefore excluded them from archaeological study. Indeed, Childe defined a culture as a class of objects "repeatedly and exclusively" found in association. More recently, Taylor (1948: 102-9) has discussed at length a grouping approach that attempts to account for all artifacts—including idiosyncratic specimens.

But the values which may be realized from an independent statistical examination of each observed variable, followed by an investigation of the degree of correlation among these variables, have not been fully explored. Spaulding (1960b: 66-71) has asserted that this kind of statistical treatment of archaeological data is the most powerful and economical and provides the most complete description possible for that data. Justification for statistical description and analysis of archaeological data lies in an anthropological interest in the cultural processes which are activated in the production and utilization of artifacts. These processes regulate centralizing tendencies in artifact production and are, in turn, predicated upon material restrictions and cultural needs. The operation of modifying tendencies will cause individual specimens to vary from the mean and will influence the distribution of values for any single variable or combination of variables. Statistical treatment will not only reveal the presence of this variation within the data but it will also measure its extent.

The descriptions which follow focus attention upon the central value of each variable together with the range and degree of normal variation exhibited by each. These values are discussed individually for each site and for convenience are condensed in Tables 5 - 8 and Figures 11 - 24. A number of summarizing quantities are introduced and expressed symbolically. These are:

$$\bar{X} = \frac{\Sigma fX}{N}$$

the sample mean, the average value of a set of values for a variable.

$$d = i\sqrt{\frac{\Sigma fx^2}{N} - \left(\frac{\Sigma fx}{N}\right)^2}$$

the standard deviation of a set of values about its mean—68% of all cases in a set fall within one standard deviation of the mean.

$$e = \frac{d}{\sqrt{N-1}}$$

the standard error of the sample mean about the probable population mean.

R = the high and low scores for a set of values for a variable.

I = the modal interval, the value range within which the greatest proportion of cases in a series occurs.

where: X = interval mid-point

f = frequency of occurence of values grouped into incremental intervals.

x = deviation of each interval mid-point from the assumed mean.

N = number of instances of variable being considered.

i = interval size.

These summarizing measurements are only applicable in those cases in which values vary quantitatively along a continuous scale (as in the case of measurements of length).

## Material

Table 3 presents the distribution of the several kinds of raw materials found at each site as a proportion of the total sample for that site. It also indicates the proportion of all tools and tool fragments made from the different materials at each site. In addition, the proportional distribution of cortex, primary, and trimming flakes in the total sample from each site is given.

The designations *chalcedony, chert, quartzite, basalt* are somewhat ambiguous and should perhaps have been abandoned in favor of less generic terms. As used here, *chalcedony* designates any very fine-grained, glassy, semi-transparent, or translucent silica rock which exhibits excellent conchoidal fracturing properties and smooth, greasy-looking fracture surfaces. The finer agates, moss-agates, and opaline rocks fall into this category. *Chert* refers to a wide range of materials in which are included "flint," "jasper," and similar cryptocrystalline rocks. These rocks are fine- to medium-grained, semi-translucent, or opaque with good conchoidal fracturing properties. Fracture surfaces are smooth but generally not greasy-looking. Cherts intergrade with the chalcedonies at one end of their spectrum and with quartzites on the other. The term *quartzite* refers to a series of course-textured rocks which have larger crystalline structures than have chalcedonies or cherts. Quartzites are metamorphic in origin and frequently the sandy composition of the parent material is visually and tactically apparent. This material is completely opaque. *Basalt* includes several dark, fine-grained igneous rocks.

*Cortex flakes* are those which retain, in over 50 per cent or more of their dorsal faces, the original outer surface of the nodule from which they were struck. The cortex has a weathered, crusty character in contrast to the "fresh" appearance of the inner material. *Primary flakes* are those which were struck from a decorticated core. *Trimming flakes* result from core rejuvenation and from secondary modification of primary flakes.

A number of general statements may be made about the data presented in Table 3. At every site, except Vernon, where chalcedonies occur, the proportion of tools made from these materials exceeds the proportional representation of chalcedony in the total sample. The opposite is true of the quartzites. No consistent pattern is exhibited by the cherts. Basalt is essentially absent from all but two sites and forms a significant component of the assemblage in only one (Vernon).

## TABLE 3

### Proportional Frequencies of Raw Materials and Flake Types

| Site | N | Chal. | Cht. | Qtz. | Bst. | Cort. | Prim. | Trim. |
|---|---|---|---|---|---|---|---|---|
| LINDENMEIER: | | | | | | | | |
| Total sample | 747 | .20 | .54 | .26 | .00 | .05 | .56 | .39 |
| Tools & Frags. | 294 | .26 | .61 | .13 | .00 | | | |
| BLACKWATER: | | | | | | | | |
| Total sample | 118 | .00 | .73 | .27 | .00 | .00 | .33 | .67 |
| Tools & Frags. | 62 | .00 | .75 | .25 | .00 | | | |
| HORNER: | | | | | | | | |
| Total sample | 120 | .13 | .68 | .19 | .00 | .01 | .30 | .69 |
| Tools & Frags. | 92 | .20 | .69 | .11 | .00 | | | |
| LEVI: | | | | | | | | |
| Total sample | 139 | .00 | 1.00 | .00 | .00 | .12 | .25 | .63 |
| Tools & Frags. | 70 | .00 | 1.00 | .00 | .00 | | | |
| SHOOP: | | | | | | | | |
| Total sample | 295 | .00 | 1.00 | .00 | .00 | .00 | .80 | .20 |
| Tools & Frags. | 157 | .00 | 1.00 | .00 | .00 | | | |
| WILLIAMSON: | | | | | | | | |
| Total sample | 186 | .01 | .95 | .04 | .00 | .16 | .53 | .31 |
| Tools & Frags. | 66 | .08 | .88 | .04 | .00 | | | |
| QUAD: | | | | | | | | |
| Total sample | 444 | .00 | .94 | .04 | .02 | — | — | — |
| Tools & Frags. | 250 | .00 | .95 | .05 | .00 | | | |
| VERNON: | | | | | | | | |
| Total sample | 198 | .07 | .58 | .03 | .32 | .10 | .54 | .36 |
| Tools & Frags. | 89 | .00 | .84 | .01 | .15 | | | |

N = number of specimens  
Chal. = chalcedony  
Cht. = chert  
Qtz. = quartzite  
Bst. = basalt  
Cort. = cortex flakes  
Prim. = primary flakes  
Trim. = trimming flakes  
Frags. = fragments

If we turn now to a consideration of the raw material composition of the individual assemblages, we will be able to examine the details behind the data summarized in the table. At Lindenmeier, a great deal of diversity characterizes those materials subsumed here under the headings *chalcedony* and *chert*. It seems likely that the different stones were imported into the site from a number of different source locations. No attempt was made to identify these locations but Coffin (1937; 1951) offers some suggestions. Coffin (1937: 10) also states that deposits of a semi-transparent chalcedony and of red quartzite are available near the site. It is significant, therefore that over 75 per cent of all cortex flakes in the sample drawn for study are of these materials. The Lindenmeier sample also includes one obsidian and one basalt specimen.

It can be said with confidence that all the specimens found at Blackwater were imported; the area is lithologically well known and there is no locally available stone that is suitable for flaking. Approximately one-third of the Blackwater material is from the Alibates Quarry near Amarillo, Texas, a source about 100 miles from the site. The bulk of the material at the Horner Site also seems to be imported—some from Shell Canyon, Wyoming approximately 60 miles away. Almost all of the collected inventory from the Shoop Site is Onondaga Chert imported from quarries that are perhaps 200 miles away. Note the absence or scarcity of cortex flakes at these sites.

The Levi Site is unlike those just discussed in that it has yielded local materials only. High quality flints and cherts are abundant in the nearby stream beds and these were extensively used at the site. The Williamson Site is also characterized by a local chert of medium quality which apparently was available in large nodules and boulders. Both of these sites yielded relatively high proportions of cortex flakes.

The presence of basalt in significantly large quantity in the Vernon collection sets this sample apart from all of the others in this study. The origins of the cherts found at the Vernon Site are not known but basalt is available locally. The relatively high incidence of cortex flakes at the site suggests that local materials were utilized. Most of those cortex flakes are basalt.

The artifacts from the Quad Site are made from a wide variety of chert materials whose origins are not known.

## Striking Platform Characteristics

Table 4 summarizes the quantitative data obtained from striking platforms. The frequencies of occurrence of the various kinds of platform preparation and of platform abrasion are given as proportions of the total number of artifacts from which these data could be obtained for each site. These totals are indicated by the N values given for each site. The mean ($\bar{X}$) and standard deviation (d) for the platform dimensions $t$ and $w$ are also shown in Table 4. Neither of these dimensions were obtained from the Blackwater and Shoop collections and only $t$ was measured for Quad.

Notice that these data may be divided into three well-defined groups. The first group, Lindenmeier, Blackwater, and Horner, exhibits a high proportion of transverse preparation, a high relative frequency of platform abrasion, and relatively small platforms. More than half of all platforms in this group were prepared transversely (from the outer edge toward the center of the core). Approximately one-third of the platforms in each of the samples in this group are abraded on their dorsal edges. In some cases, this abrasion extends over the entire surface of the platform and in a few specimens it occurs beyond the limits of the platform. Frequency of abrasion was compared with raw material type in the Lindenmeier sample. The results indicate that all of the material types present in this sample were abraded with essentially the same frequency (chalcedony 40 per cent, chert 37 per cent, quartzite 37 per cent).

The second group consists of the Levi, Shoop, Williamson, and Quad samples. The relationship between transverse and flat preparation in this group is the reverse of that found in the first group of samples. Flat preparation is exhibited by about 60 per cent of the specimens in the four samples now being considered. Lateral preparation is also more frequent in all of these samples except that from Shoop. Platform abrasion, except in the Williamson sample, is considerably less frequent than it is in the Lindenmeier, Blackwater, and Horner samples; indeed it is all but absent from the Levi sample. Platform size in this second group is relatively large.

The third group consists of the Vernon sample alone. Notice that while the frequency of flat preparation remains relatively high, lateral preparation accounts for nearly one-third of this sample. This is in strong contrast to the other samples in the survey. The frequency of platform abrasion remains relatively low and compares to that of Shoop and Quad. Abrasion occurs as frequently on basalt specimens (15 per cent occurrence) as it does in all other materials in the sample. Platform size is relatively small in the Vernon sample.

## Flake Angle

The distribution of values of $<\beta$ obtained for the eight sites under consideration is presented in Figures 11 - 14. The summarizing statistics for this variable in each sample are also indicated. Four of these distributions, those for Lindenmeier, Blackwater, Horner, and Levi, are strongly unimodal in the same interval

## TABLE 4

### Striking Platform Characteristics

| Site | Trns. | Flt. | Mlt. | Lat. | Abrs. | t | w |
|---|---|---|---|---|---|---|---|
| LINDENMEIER: N = 597 | .51 | .39 | .04 | .06 | .38 | $\bar{X}$ = 3.13<br>d = 2.07 | 7.25<br>2.24 |
| BLACKWATER: N = 64 | .76 | .16 | .02 | .06 | .34 | $\bar{X}$ = —<br>d = — | —<br>— |
| HORNER: N = 66 | .66 | .28 | .00 | .06 | .32 | $\bar{X}$ = 3.53<br>d = 2.29 | 7.44<br>2.57 |
| LEVI: N = 108 | .27 | .56 | .07 | .10 | .02 | $\bar{X}$ = 6.88<br>d = 3.02 | 9.99<br>0 |
| SHOOP: N = 160 | .35 | .61 | .00 | .04 | .16 | $\bar{X}$ = —<br>d = — | —<br>— |
| WILLIAMSON: N = 153 | .29 | .58 | .00 | .13 | .28 | $\bar{X}$ = 4.44<br>d = 2.51 | 8.29<br>2.33 |
| QUAD: N = 336 | .24 | .59 | .08 | .09 | .12 | $\bar{X}$ = 4.28<br>d = 2.44 | —<br>— |
| VERNON: N = 157 | .22 | .45 | .02 | .31 | .16 | $\bar{X}$ = 3.50<br>d = 2.26 | 7.24<br>2.48 |

Trns. = transverse  
Flt. = flat  
Mlt. = multilateral  
Lat. = lateral  
Abrs. = abrasion  
t = transverse length  
w = lateral length  
N = number of specimens  
$\bar{X}$ = mean value  
d = standard deviation  

(68° - 71°). Two others, Shoop and Williamson, are also unimodal but, in this case, I = 72° - 75°. The other two sites, Quad and Vernon, display bimodal distributions which share the same I values (72° - 75° and 80° - 83°).

The samples may be assigned to two groups with respect to the mean value of $<\beta$. In one group, this value falls between 67° and 69°; in the other, it is more closely defined between 72° and 73°. As will be seen later in this chapter, this difference, though small, is significant. The Lindenmeier, Blackwater, Horner, and Levi samples are in the former category. Shoop, Williamson, Quad, and Vernon belong in the latter group. Notice, however, that the most general statement that can be made about the behavior of this variable in these eight samples is that, regardless

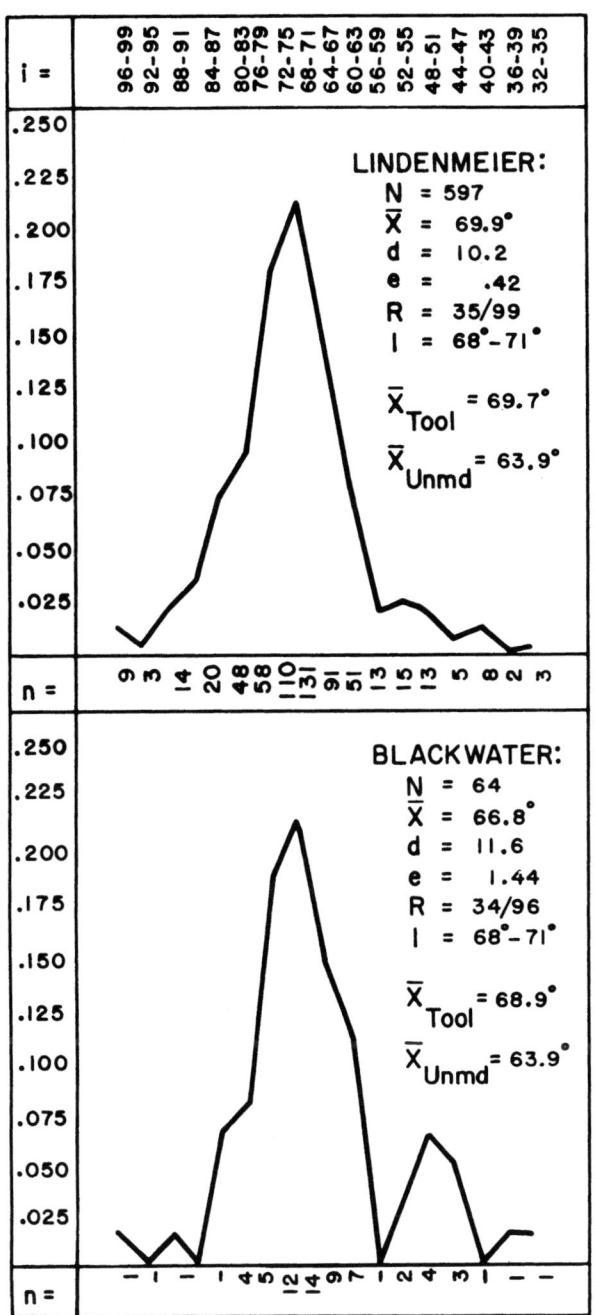

Fig. 11. Proportional frequency distributions of $<\beta$ for Lindenmeier and Blackwater.

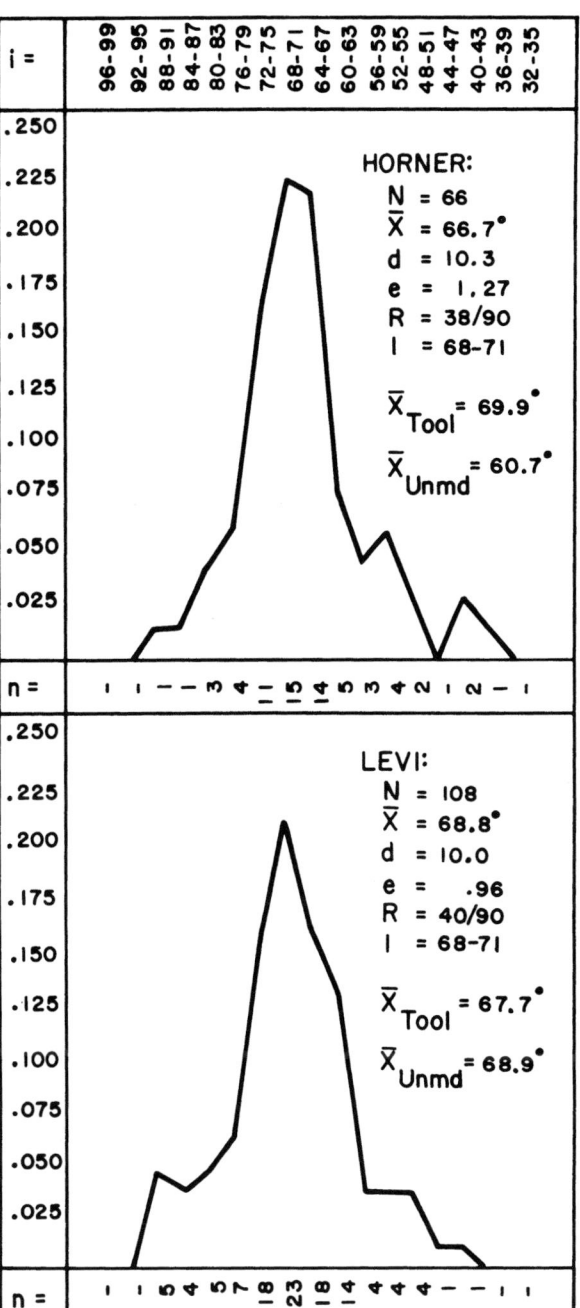

Fig. 12. Proportional frequency distributions of $<\beta$ for Horner and Levi.

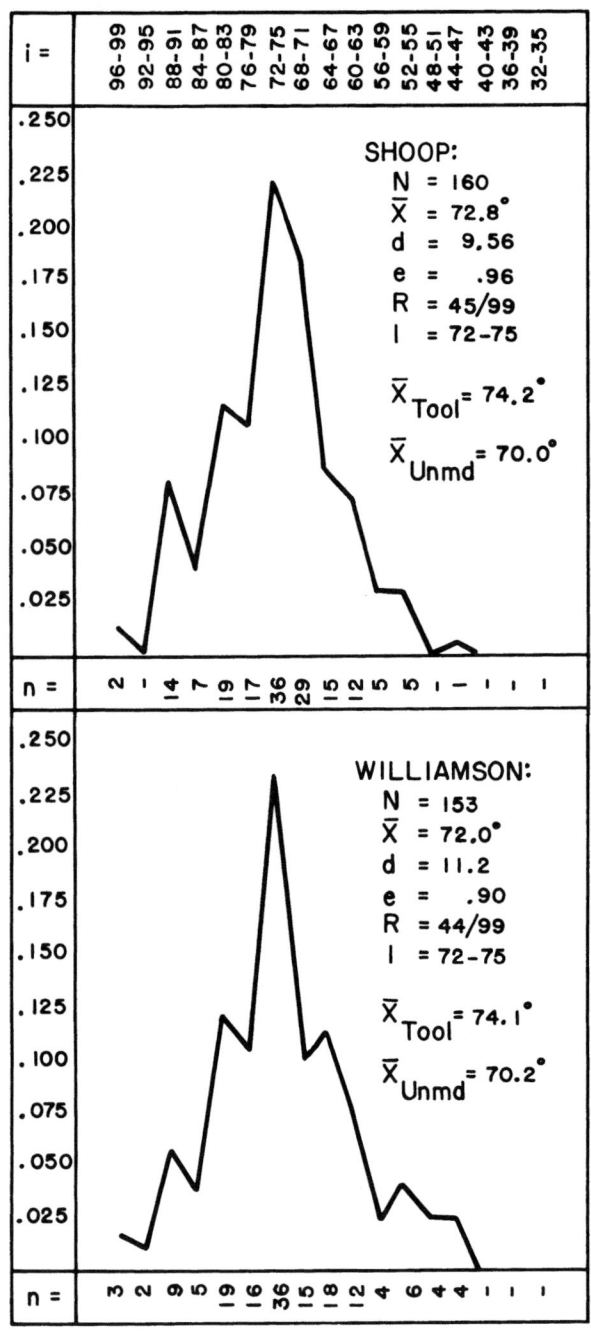

Fig. 13. Proportional frequency distributions of $<\beta$ for Shoop and Williamson.

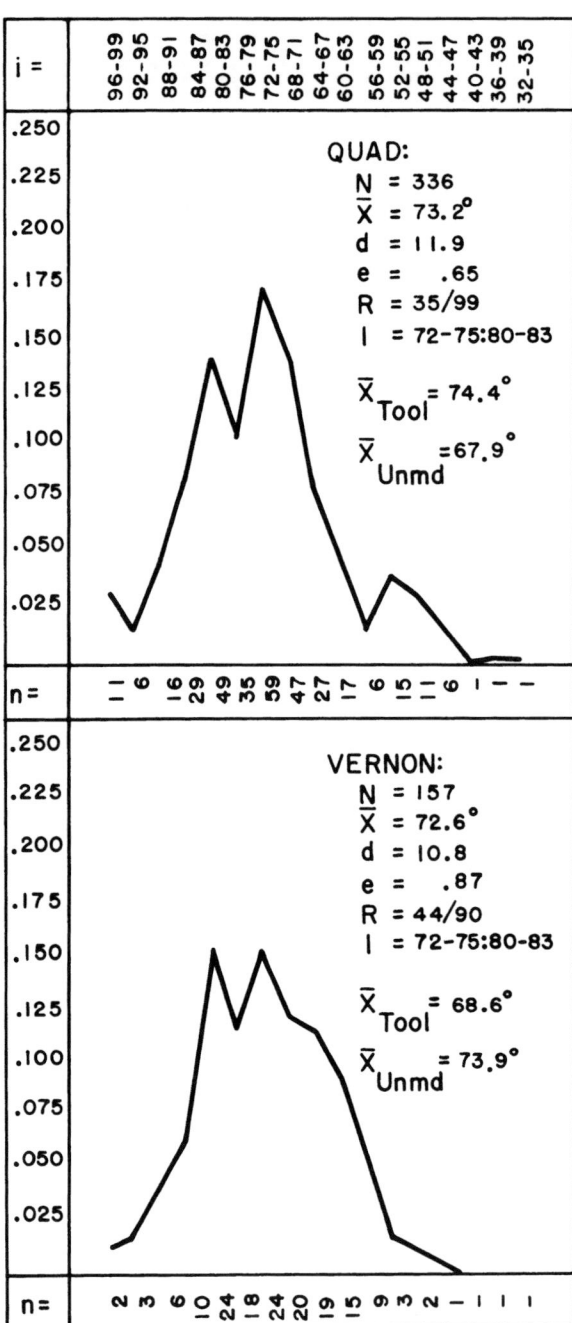

Fig. 14. Proportional frequency distributions of $<\beta$ for Quad and Vernon.

of the specific values of $\bar{X}$ and of I displayed by each sample, in all cases (except one) the mean value of $<\beta$ found on tools falls within the modal interval value of $<\beta$ for that sample. The sole exception is Vernon, where $\bar{X}_{Tool}$ is smaller than I. It may be significant, in view of the fact that both sites have yielded Folsom points, that the mean value of this variable at Vernon compares favorably with the corresponding quantity for Lindenmeier. Furthermore, with the exception of those for the Vernon and Levi samples, the values $\bar{X}_{Tool}$ are always greater than the values $\bar{X}_{Flake}$.

If we examine the distribution graphs for specifically shared traits among the samples, we find that three of the sites, Lindemeier, Blackwater, and Horner, are relatively well represented on the low end of the scale. About 15 per cent of the values at each of these sites is within the lower third of the scale. Indeed, representation in this range is so great in the latter two samples that $\bar{X}_\beta$ values for these samples are the lowest in the entire group. However, note that sample sizes are very small for both the Blackwater and Horner sites and that $\bar{X}_\beta$ values for tools at these sites compare favorably with $\bar{X}_\beta$ Lindenmeier. The smallness of the samples probably accounts for the low values of $\bar{X}_\beta$ and for the skewed distribution of this variable at these sites.

Four of the samples are relatively strong in high values of $<\beta$. These are Shoop, Williamson, Quad, and Vernon. At each of these sites, about 30 per cent of the values recorded for this variable occur within the upper third of the scale. These are the same four samples from which higher values of $\bar{X}_\beta$ were obtained. It should be noted that these higher values reflect a real quantitative shift toward less acute values of $<\beta$ and are not simply a reflection of overrepresentation of any specific interval of high values. The N values for all four of these samples are reasonably large and in the Quad sample, N reaches the second highest value in the entire series. There is a tendency for the most acute values of $<\beta$ to be truncated but in the Quad sample, with the highest recorded $\bar{X}$ value (73.2°), there is a full range of variation within this variable.

A final statement may be made about these data. The Lindenmeier sample was tested for differences in the mean value of $<\beta$ recorded for the three principle raw material categories found at that site. There were none: $\bar{X}_{sample} = 69.9°$; $\bar{X}_{chal.} = 70.0°$; $\bar{X}_{cht.} = 69.4°$; $\bar{X}_{qtz.} = 68.6°$. The basalt component at Vernon was also tested with identical results: $\bar{X}_{sample} = 72.6°$; $\bar{X}_{bst.} = 71.1°$.

## The Medial Axis

The distribution of and summary quantities for values of $<\alpha$ are presented in Figures 15 and 16. The fact that the modal interval of incidence for this measurement is the same for each site is of interest. Nevertheless, a number of differences in the distributions of values of this variable among the sites should be noted. The mean value of $<\alpha$ obtained for the Quad sample is 8.4; this value is relatively large compared to those for the other samples. The Quad sample also differs from the others in that the value of $<\alpha$ exceeds 19° on 6 per cent of the specimens in this sample. In all of the other samples this value is reached or exceeded by only 2 per cent or less of the specimens. The Vernon sample differs from all the others in the relatively high proportion of 0° values which are indicated for this variable.

The mean value of $<\alpha_{Tool}$ for three samples— Lindenmeier, Blackwater, Horner—is within the modal interval of this measurement in these samples. The value of $\bar{X}_{Tool}$ in two other samples—Levi and Shoop—falls outside the I values for these samples by only one-half of a degree. These differences are too small to have any real significance as indicators of site differences. The three remaining sites— Williamson, Quad, and Vernon—exhibit $\bar{X}_{Tool}$ values that are greater than 7°. This is, again, only a small deviation from I; but, in view of the small values being considered, it may be worth testing the significance of the differences between these values and those obtained for the Lindenmeier - Blackwater - Horner group.

## Artifact Dimensions

Length, width, and thickness data obtained from the various samples are presented in Tables 5, 6, and 7. Three ratio values for each sample also appear in these tables. These ratios are: width-length (W/L), thickness-width (T/W), and thickness-length (T/L).

Specimens in the Levi and Quad samples tend to be appreciably longer than those in the other samples taken as wholes and this tendency persists in the tool and utilized flake categories of these two samples.

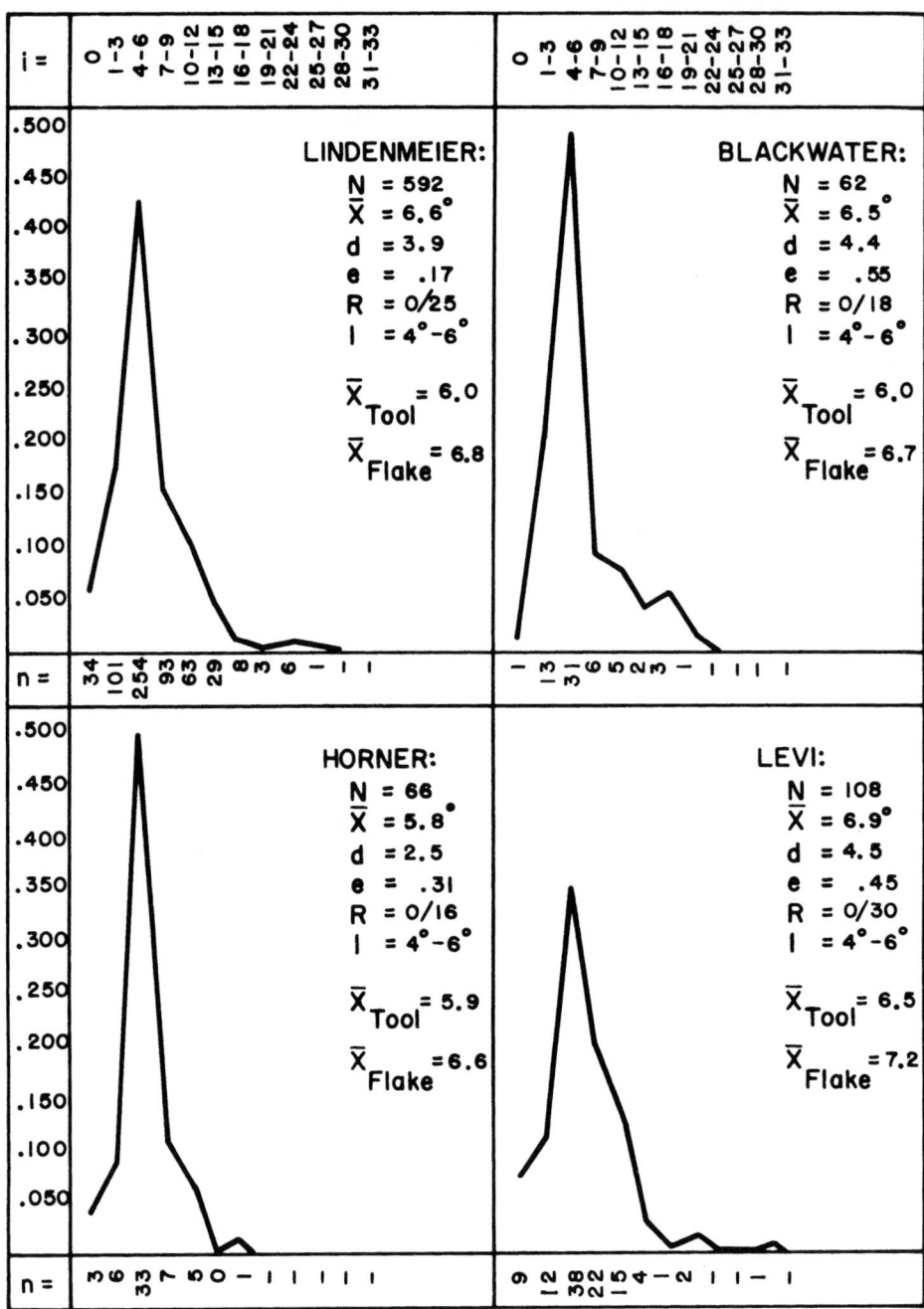

Fig. 15. Proportional frequency distributions of $<\alpha$ for Lindenmeier, Blackwater, Horner, and Levi.

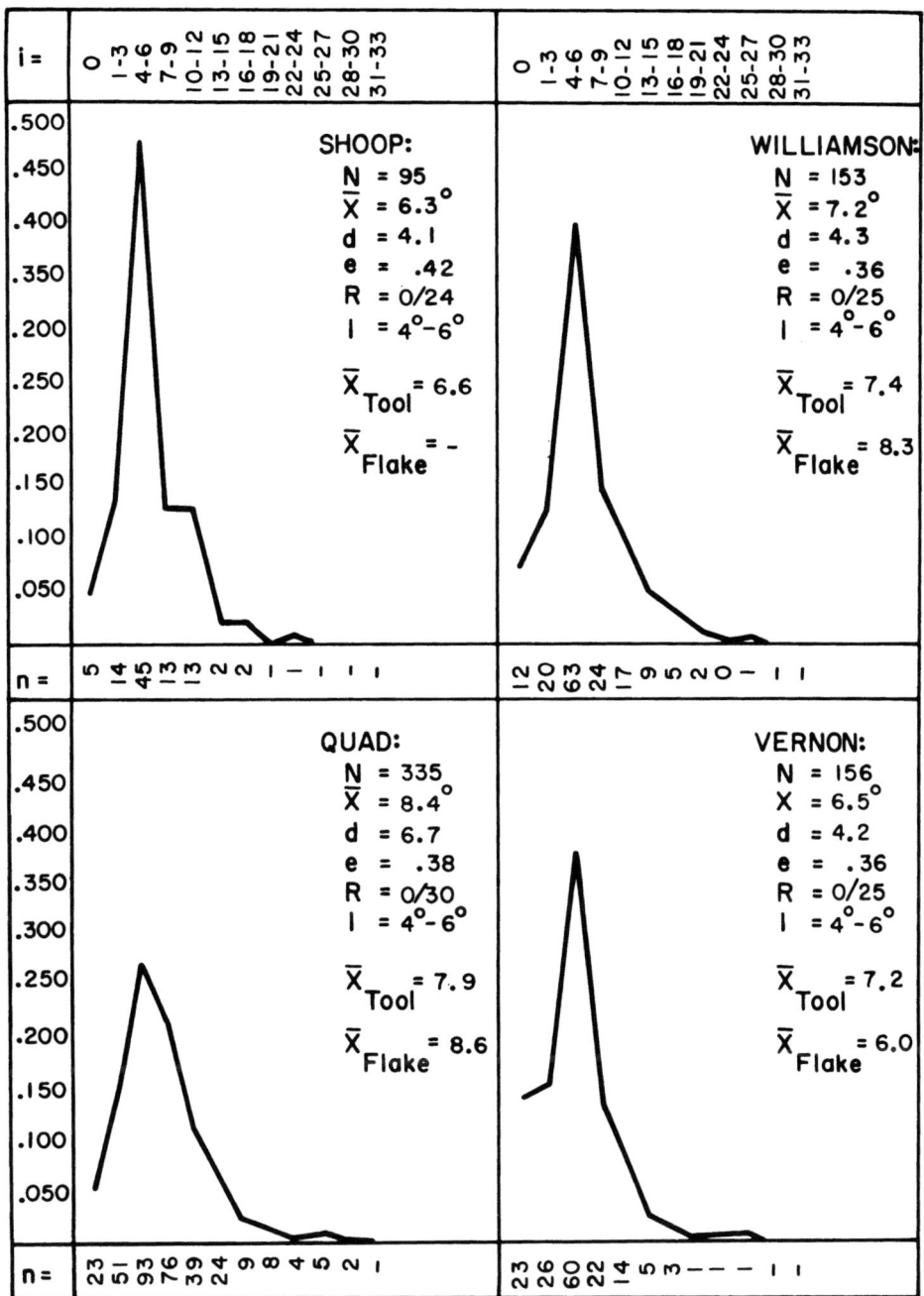

Fig. 16. Proportional frequency distributions of $<\alpha$ for Shoop, Williamson, Quad, and Vernon.

## TABLE 5

### Mean Values of Length (mm) and Width-Length Ratios

| Site | N | $\bar{X}$ | d | e | R | W/L |
|---|---|---|---|---|---|---|
| **LINDENMEIER:** | | | | | | |
|   Total sample | 578 | 43.63 | 16.37 | 0.98 | 18–99 | .72 |
|   Tools | 158 | 43.07 | 17.38 | 1.38 | | |
|   Flakes | 120 | 49.27 | 17.58 | 2.97 | | |
| **BLACKWATER:** | | | | | | |
|   Total sample | 118 | 44.59 | 19.35 | 1.76 | 11–99 | .69 |
|   Tools | — | — | — | — | | |
|   Flakes | — | — | — | — | | |
| **HORNER:** | | | | | | |
|   Total sample | 91 | 33.79 | 14.06 | 1.47 | 15–99 | .78 |
|   Tools | 28 | 37.16 | 14.72 | 2.78 | | |
|   Flakes | 26 | 38.96 | 16.98 | 3.33 | | |
| **LEVI:** | | | | | | |
|   Total sample | 70 | 55.04 | 17.28 | 2.07 | 27–96 | .77 |
|   Tools | 41 | 61.12 | 16.00 | 2.50 | | |
|   Flakes | 17 | 48.38 | 17.29 | 4.19 | | |
| **SHOOP:** | | | | | | |
|   Total sample | 132 | 28.38 | 9.02 | 0.79 | 11–64 | .75 |
|   Tools | — | — | — | — | | |
|   Flakes | — | — | — | — | | |
| **WILLIAMSON:** | | | | | | |
|   Total sample | 181 | 41.21 | 15.29 | 1.14 | 18–99 | .74 |
|   Tools | 45 | 41.89 | 15.56 | 2.32 | | |
|   Flakes | 10 | 38.50 | 13.35 | 4.22 | | |
| **QUAD:** | | | | | | |
|   Total sample | 444 | 49.05 | 13.69 | 0.65 | 20–99 | .63 |
|   Tools | 210 | 52.51 | 13.48 | 0.93 | | |
|   Flakes | 58 | 48.66 | 14.32 | 1.88 | | |
| **VERNON:** | | | | | | |
|   Total sample | 196 | 28.98 | 13.93 | 0.99 | 11–78 | .82 |
|   Tools | 12 | 50.79 | 18.83 | 5.44 | | |
|   Flakes | 67 | 32.49 | 11.89 | 1.45 | | |

Tools = whole tools only
Flakes = utilized flakes only
W/L = width divided by length

# TABLE 6

## Mean Values of Width (mm) and Frequency of Incidence of Maximum Width Position Values

| Site | N | $\bar{X}$ | d | e | R | max W pos 0–2 | max W pos 3 | max W pos 4–6 |
|---|---|---|---|---|---|---|---|---|
| **LINDENMEIER:** | | | | | | | | |
| Total sample | 578 | 31.50 | 11.06 | 0.66 | 11–81 | .20 | .40 | .40 |
| Tools | 158 | 31.67 | 10.67 | 0.85 | | .04 | .25 | .71 |
| Flakes | 120 | 36.14 | 15.17 | 2.57 | | | | |
| **BLACKWATER:** | | | | | | | | |
| Total sample | 118 | 29.16 | 12.41 | 1.14 | 8–52 | — | — | — |
| Tools | — | — | — | — | | — | — | — |
| Flakes | — | — | — | — | | | | |
| **HORNER:** | | | | | | | | |
| Total sample | 91 | 26.44 | 8.41 | 0.88 | 14–54 | .08 | .42 | .50 |
| Tools | 28 | 27.16 | 7.29 | 1.38 | | .04 | .25 | .71 |
| Flakes | 26 | 31.42 | 10.62 | 2.08 | | | | |
| **LEVI:** | | | | | | | | |
| Total sample | 70 | 42.61 | 13.33 | 1.59 | 22–92 | .20 | .42 | .38 |
| Tools | 41 | 44.78 | 12.85 | 2.01 | | .31 | .38 | .31 |
| Flakes | 17 | 39.38 | 15.86 | 3.85 | | | | |
| **SHOOP:** | | | | | | | | |
| Total sample | 132 | 21.53 | 6.13 | 0.53 | 7–39 | — | — | — |
| Tools | — | — | — | — | | — | — | — |
| Flakes | — | — | — | — | | | | |
| **WILLIAMSON:** | | | | | | | | |
| Total sample | 181 | 30.29 | 10.95 | 0.81 | 16–80 | .32 | .23 | .45 |
| Tools | 45 | 29.96 | 12.28 | 1.83 | | .11 | .16 | .73 |
| Flakes | 10 | 38.50 | 13.35 | 4.22 | | | | |
| **QUAD:** | | | | | | | | |
| Total sample | 444 | 31.06 | 9.48 | 0.45 | 13–82 | — | — | — |
| Tools | 210 | 31.12 | 9.20 | 0.64 | | .23 | .41 | .36 |
| Flakes | 58 | 30.83 | 13.91 | 1.82 | | | | |
| **VERNON:** | | | | | | | | |
| Total sample | 196 | 23.85 | 9.80 | 0.70 | 10–59 | .31 | .39 | .30 |
| Tools | 12 | 36.92 | 15.00 | 4.33 | | .08 | .38 | .54 |
| Flakes | 67 | 26.37 | 10.22 | 1.25 | | | | |

max W pos = maximum width position  
Tools = whole tools only  
Flakes = utilized flakes only

## TABLE 7

### Mean Values of Thickness (mm) and Thickness Ratios

| Site | N | $\bar{X}$ | d | e | R | T/L | T/W |
|---|---|---|---|---|---|---|---|
| **LINDENMEIER:** | | | | | | | |
| Total sample | 578 | 8.00 | 3.43 | 0.21 | 1–26 | .18 | .25 |
| Tools | 158 | 7.89 | 2.97 | 0.27 | | | |
| Flakes | 120 | 9.20 | 5.20 | 0.88 | | | |
| **BLACKWATER:** | | | | | | | |
| Total sample | 118 | 5.86 | 3.90 | 0.36 | 1–17 | .13 | .20 |
| Tools | — | — | — | — | | | |
| Flakes | — | — | — | — | | | |
| **HORNER:** | | | | | | | |
| Total sample | 91 | 6.80 | 2.59 | 0.27 | 3–15 | .20 | .25 |
| Tools | 28 | 7.05 | 2.62 | 0.49 | | | |
| Flakes | 26 | 7.73 | 3.19 | 0.63 | | | |
| **LEVI:** | | | | | | | |
| Total sample | 70 | 12.76 | 6.28 | 0.75 | 3–31 | .23 | .30 |
| Tools | 41 | 13.01 | 5.61 | 0.88 | | | |
| Flakes | 17 | 10.77 | 7.24 | 1.76 | | | |
| **SHOOP:** | | | | | | | |
| Total sample | 132 | 6.76 | 2.47 | 0.21 | 3–22 | .24 | .31 |
| Tools | — | — | — | — | | | |
| Flakes | — | — | — | — | | | |
| **WILLIAMSON:** | | | | | | | |
| Total sample | 181 | 8.85 | 4.43 | 0.33 | 3–29 | .21 | .29 |
| Tools | 45 | 10.17 | 4.44 | 0.66 | | | |
| Flakes | 10 | 13.15 | 4.42 | 1.40 | | | |
| **QUAD:** | | | | | | | |
| Total sample | 444 | 8.57 | 3.26 | 0.16 | 1–27 | .18 | .27 |
| Tools | 210 | 9.22 | 3.26 | 0.23 | | | |
| Flakes | 58 | 7.58 | 3.98 | 0.52 | | | |
| **VERNON:** | | | | | | | |
| Total sample | 196 | 7.00 | 4.71 | 0.34 | 2–34 | .24 | .29 |
| Tools | 12 | 15.04 | 9.00 | 2.60 | | | |
| Flakes | 67 | 8.08 | 4.39 | 0.54 | | | |

Tools = whole tools only
Flakes = utilized flakes only
T/L = thickness divided by length
T/W = thickness divided by width

Conversely, Horner and Shoop specimens tend to be relatively short both in general and as tools (the Shoop sample consists primarily of tools; therefore, total sample values may be taken as generally indicative of tool characteristics). Notice, however, that although the mean specimen length in the Vernon sample is quite low, mean tool length is high. Inspection of the W/L values for these sites reveals a high degree of similarity between all but two of the samples. The Quad sample deviates from the others in the direction of greater elongation while the Vernon specimens tend to be more nearly equal in length and width.

The mean value of width is relatively uniform among the samples except that Levi specimens tend to be appreciably wider and Shoop specimens tend to be more narrow. The mean width of tools in each sample is approximately equal to the mean width of all specimens in that sample except at Vernon. As in the case of length, the Vernon sample contrasts a very low mean specimen width with a very high mean tool width.

The position of maximum width in the Lindenmeier, Horner, and Williamson samples tends to occur between the mid-point of a tool and its distal end. This tendency is less strongly apparent among Vernon specimens which also exhibit some tendency toward mid-point maxima. The maximum width position of tools is more uniformly distributed in the Levi and Quad samples. Notice that, in contrast to all others, these latter two samples exhibit relatively high frequencies of width maxima in the proximal halves of tools. High frequencies of location of maximum width in the proximal area characterize the total samples drawn from the Williamson and Levi Sites. The total Horner sample exhibits a very low frequency of occurrence of this variable in the proximal range.

The data presented in Table 7 indicate that all specimens in three samples—Blackwater, Horner, and Shoop—tend to be relatively thin. Tools in the Horner sample—the only one of these three for which data in this category are available—also tend to be relatively thin. The maximum thickness values recorded for these samples, and especially those for Blackwater and Horner, are relatively low. The Levi sample, in contrast, contains uniformly thick specimens. Williamson and Vernon tools also tend to be thick. The maximum thickness values recorded for these three samples are the highest obtained. The ratios of thickness to length and width reveal the fact that Levi, Williamson, and Vernon specimens tend to be thick in relation to length and width while Horner and Lindenmeier artifacts tend to be thin in relation to other dimensions. Although their absolute thicknesses are not great, Shoop artifacts tend to be at least as thick in relation to their lengths and widths as are artifacts in the Levi, Williamson, and Vernon samples. Blackwater specimens tend to be thin both in absolute terms and in relation to length and width.

## Edge Angles

The data obtained from measurements of $<\delta_L$ and $<\delta_D$ are presented in Figures 17 - 24 and in Table 8. The Blackwater and Horner samples are characterized by relatively low mean values for both lateral and distal edge angles. Neither sample contains appreciable numbers of accessory tool forms but the Horner sample displays a relatively high proportion of distal edge modification. I values for both samples are centered at 50° or less. The Lindenmeier and Quad samples exhibit relatively low mean values of $<\delta_L$ combined with relatively high mean values of $<\delta_D$. The proportion of distal edge modification and accessory tool occurrence are generally moderate in these two samples. An exception is found in the very low D value obtained for the Quad sample. The range of distribution of edge angle values is great in both the Lindenmeier and the Quad samples.

Relatively high mean values of both edge angles characterize the Shoop, Levi, and Williamson samples. All of these samples also contain high proportions of accessory tool forms and all but Levi yield high D values. The modal interval of $<\delta_D$ is 66° - 75° for all of these samples and that for $<\delta_L$ is 56° - 65° for Williamson and Levi. The Shoop sample displays a relatively broad range of edge angle values but the R values at Williamson and Levi are restricted to the higher end of the scale.

Although a number of the distributions of $<\delta_L$ tend to be more or less bimodal, only the Vernon sample (and to a lesser extent, the Quad sample) displays a bimodal distribution of $<\delta_D$. The Vernon sample is also unique in that it combines a very high frequency of tool concavities with a relatively low frequency of tips. Mean edge angle values for this sample are intermediate between the low and high value sample groups.

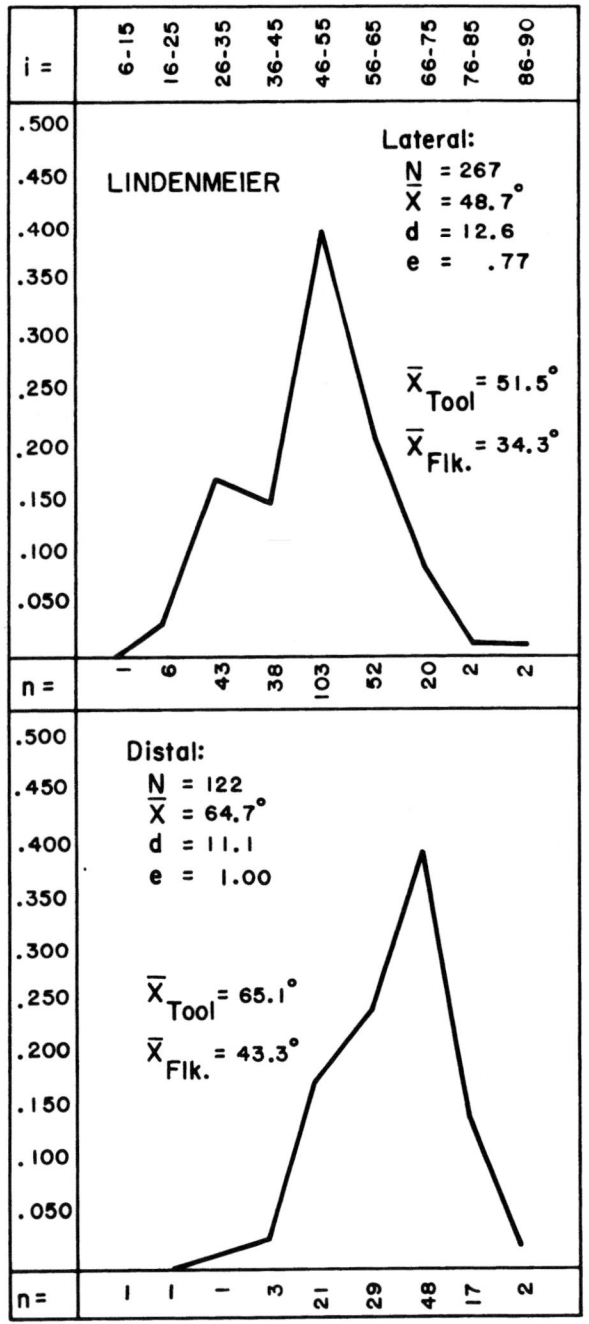

Fig. 17. Proportional frequency distributions of $<\delta_L$ and $<\delta_D$ for Lindenmeier.

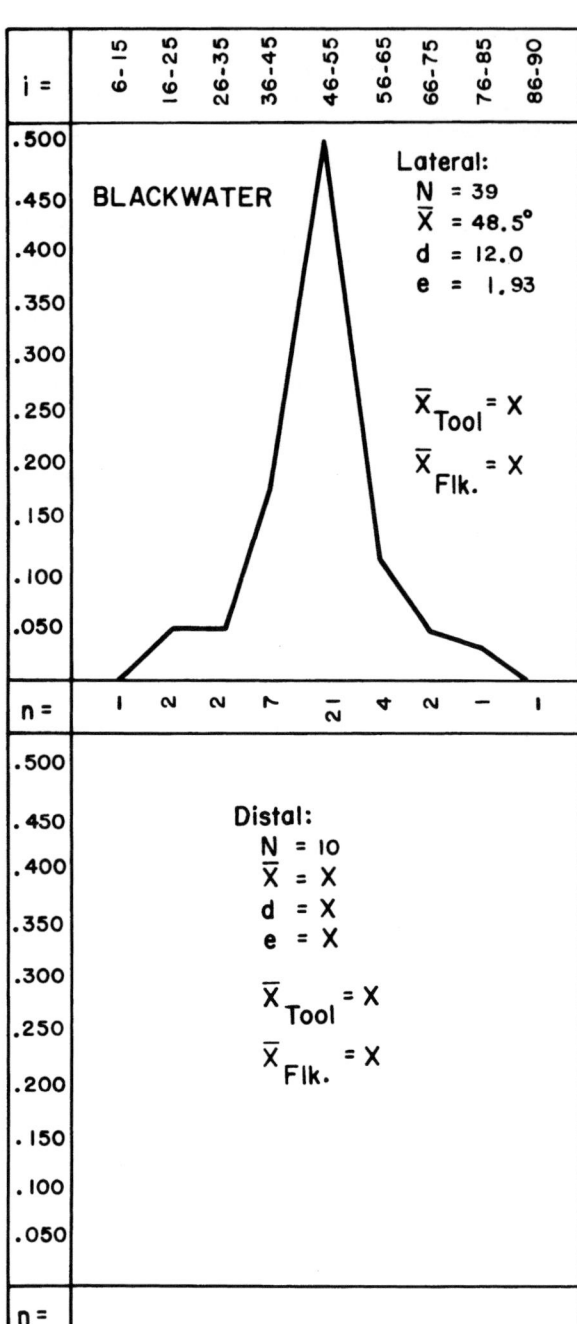

Fig. 18. Proportional frequency distribution of $<\delta_L$ for Blackwater. $<\delta_D$ based on N of 10 not adequate for plotting.

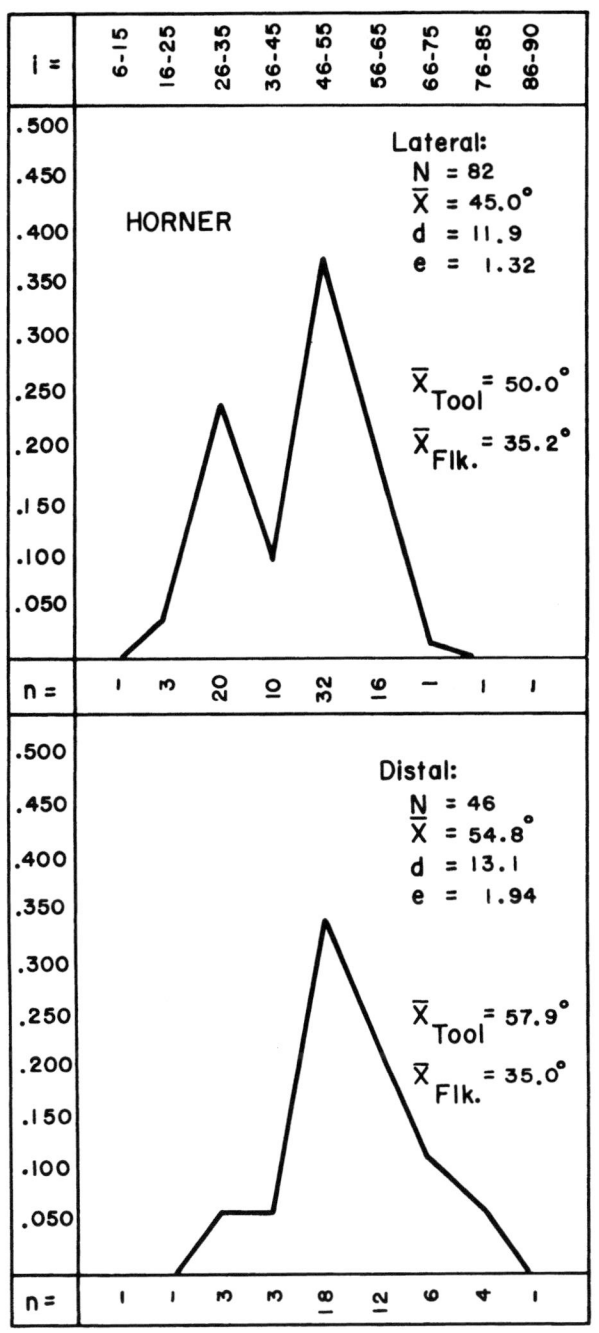

Fig. 19. Proportional frequency distribution of $<\!\delta_L$ and $<\!\delta_D$ for Horner.

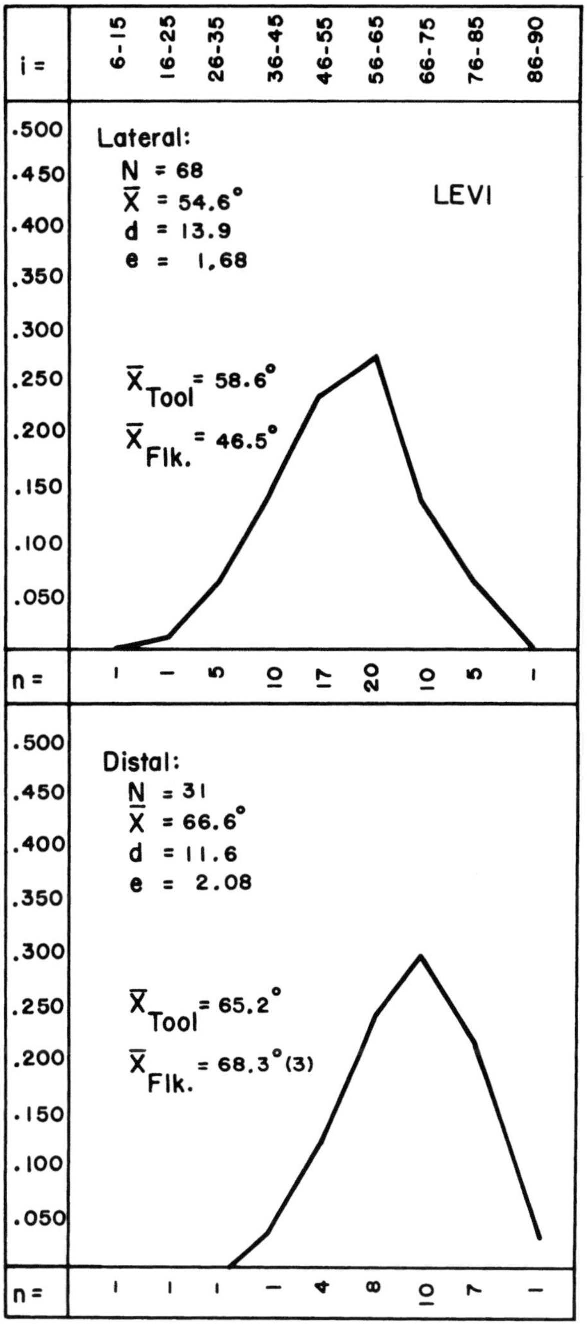

Fig. 20. Proportional frequency distribution of $<\!\delta_L$ and $<\!\delta_D$ for Levi.

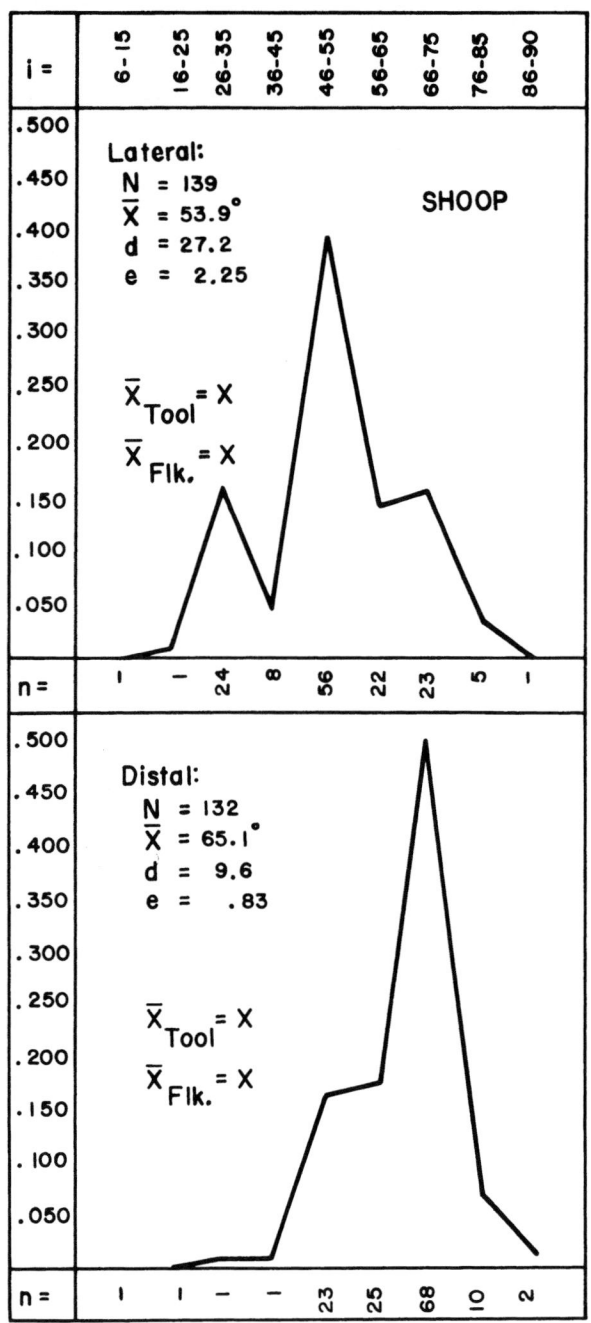

Fig. 21. Proportional frequency distribution of $<\delta_I$ and $<\delta_D$ for Shoop.

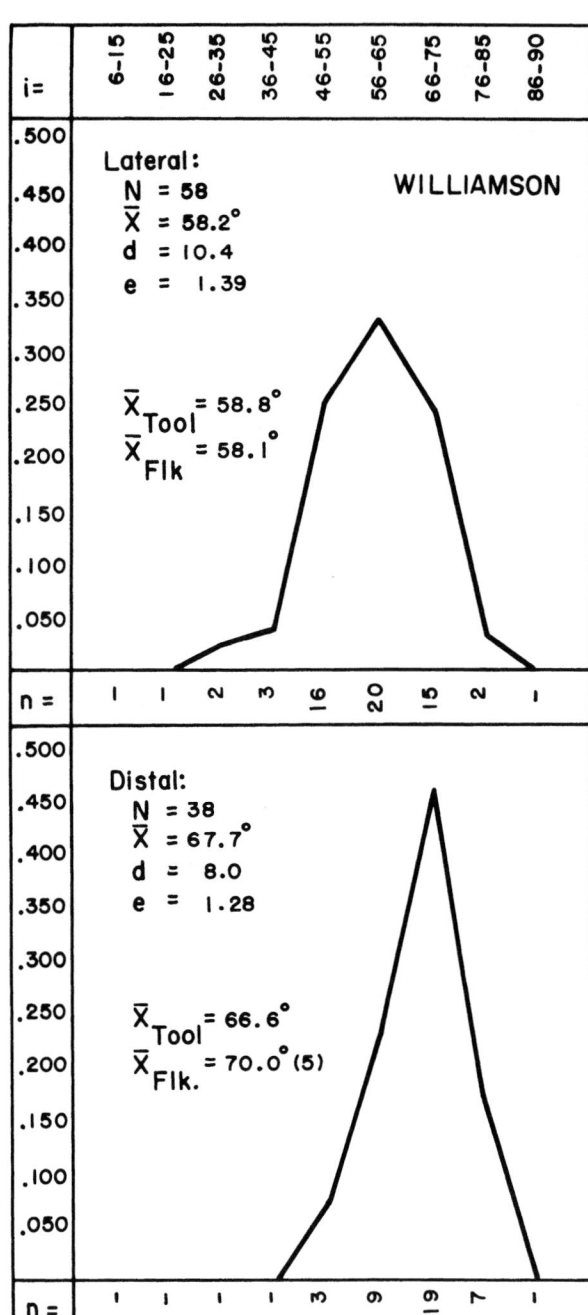

Fig. 22. Proportional frequency distribution of $<\delta_I$ and $<\delta_D$ for Williamson.

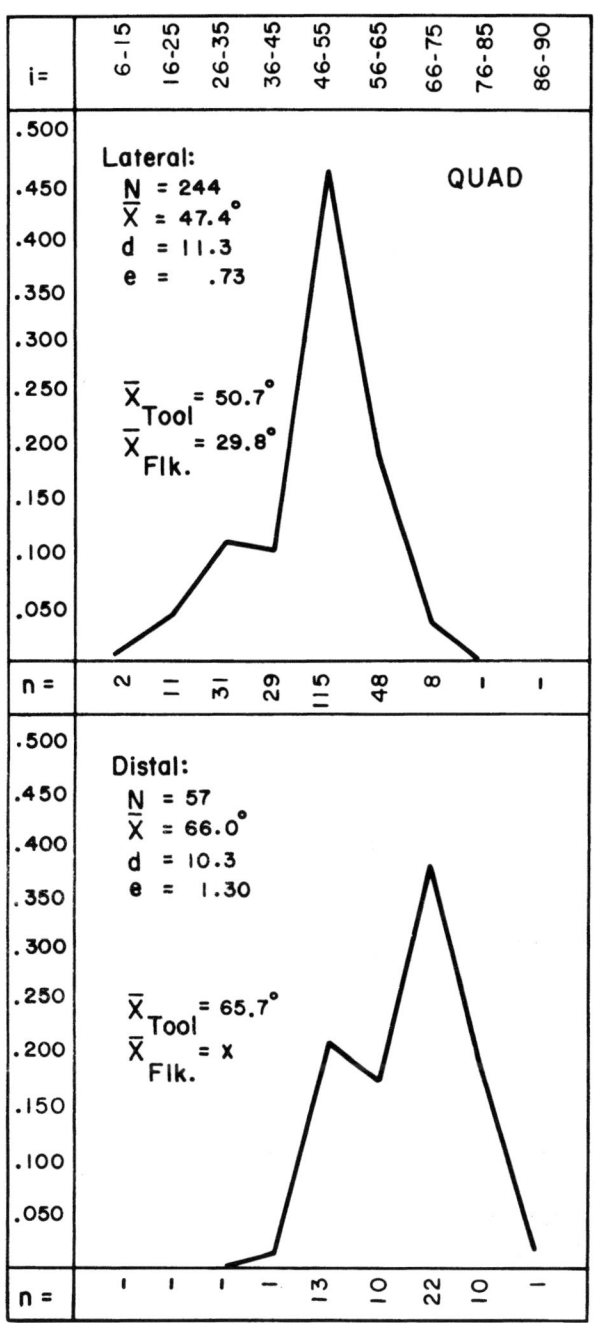

Fig. 23. Proportional frequency distribution of $<\delta_L$ and $<\delta_D$ for Quad.

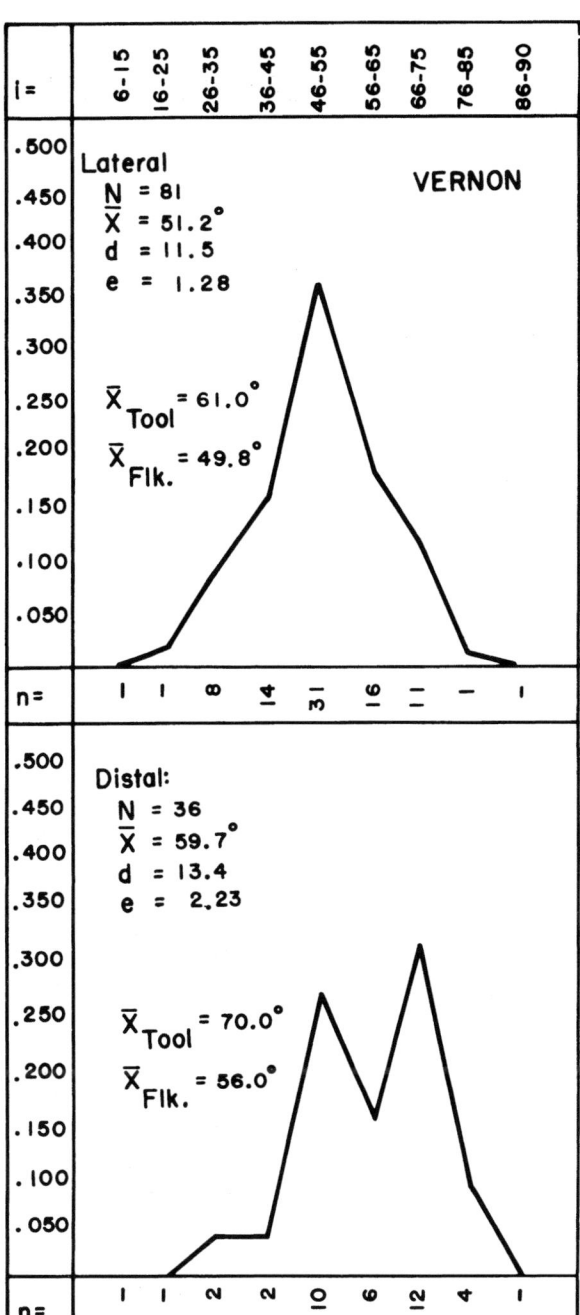

Fig. 24. Proportional frequency distribution of $<\delta_L$ and $<\delta_D$ for Vernon.

## TABLE 8

### Edge Angle Values and Frequency of Accessory Tool Forms

| Site | N | $\bar{X}\delta_L$ | $\bar{X}\delta_D$ | D | Accessories tip. | Accessories con. |
|---|---|---|---|---|---|---|
| **LINDENMEIER:** | | | | | | |
| Tools | 158 | 52.0 | 65.3 | .31 | .09 | .05 |
| Flakes | 120 | 34.3 | 43.3 | | | |
| **BLACKWATER:** | | | | | | |
| Tools | — | — | — | .21 | .03 | .03 |
| Flakes | — | — | — | | | |
| **HORNER:** | | | | | | |
| Tools | 28 | 49.5 | 58.3 | .36 | .07 | .00 |
| Flakes | 26 | 35.2 | x | | | |
| **LEVI:** | | | | | | |
| Tools | 41 | 58.6 | 65.2 | .31 | .17 | .26 |
| Flakes | 17 | 46.5 | 68.3 | | | |
| **SHOOP:** | | | | | | |
| Tools | — | — | — | .49 | .18 | .11 |
| Flakes | — | — | — | | | |
| **WILLIAMSON:** | | | | | | |
| Tools | 45 | 58.8 | 66.6 | .40 | .17 | .18 |
| Flakes | 10 | 58.1 | x | | | |
| **QUAD:** | | | | | | |
| Tools | 210 | 50.2 | 66.5 | .19 | — | — |
| Flakes | 58 | 29.9 | x | | | |
| **VERNON:** | | | | | | |
| Tools | 12 | 61.0 | 70.0 | .31 | .09 | .27 |
| Flakes | 67 | 49.9 | 56.0 | | | |

D = proportion of all specimens with distal retouch or use
tip. = proportion of all specimens with tips
con. = proportion of all specimens with concavities (including spokeshaves)
Tools = whole tools plus fragments
Flakes = utilized flakes only
x = number of cases too small to be used

## Correlations between Variables

Matrices of correlation between variables at each site are presented in Tables 10 - 15. These tables indicate the degree of correlation that exists between a variable and each of seven other variables at each site. In addition, Table 9 presents a matrix in which data from six sites have been pooled and correlated in the same way. Data obtained from the Blackwater and Shoop collections are not included in these tables because three of the variables were not recorded in a manner comparable to recording procedures used for the other six samples (p. 29). The eight variables which are correlated were all rated on a continuous,

TABLE 9

Correlations between Variables: Pooled Data

| | 1 | 2 | 3 | 4 | 5 | 6 | 7 | 8 | N | $\bar{X}$ | d |
|---|---|---|---|---|---|---|---|---|---|---|---|
| t = 1 | | .216<br>37.59 | .053<br>2.15 | .255<br>47.57 | .446<br>169.84 | .443<br>167.01 | .208<br>18.95 | .069<br>.68 | 780 | 3.9 | 2.5 |
| β = 2 | 770 | | −.008<br>.09 | .073<br>4.62 | .109<br>10.38 | .184<br>30.24 | .132<br>7.61 | .049<br>.34 | 1416 | 70.9 | 11.1 |
| α = 3 | 766 | 1406 | | .154<br>21.01 | −.010<br>.09 | .028<br>.68 | .028<br>.34 | .066<br>.63 | 1410 | 6.5 | 5.0 |
| L = 4 | 686 | 865 | 867 | | .535<br>504.86 | .569<br>602.77 | .052<br>2.12 | .043<br>.62 | 1261 | 42.8 | 16.6 |
| W = 5 | 686 | 865 | 867 | 1261 | | .600<br>708.19 | .143<br>16.29 | .065<br>1.42 | 1261 | 30.2 | 11.0 |
| T = 6 | 686 | 865 | 867 | 1261 | 1261 | | .359<br>115.55 | .240<br>20.48 | 1262 | 8.3 | 4.1 |
| δL = 7 | 421 | 431 | 432 | 782 | 782 | 783 | | .375<br>48.27 | 798 | 49.3 | 12.4 |
| δD = 8 | 144 | 143 | 145 | 336 | 336 | 337 | 297 | | 337 | 63.6 | 11.9 |

☐ $p = .001$
[ ] $p = .01$

## TABLE 10

### Correlations between Variables: Lindenmeier

|   | 1 | 2 | 3 | 4 | 5 | 6 | 7 | 8 | N | $\bar{X}$ | d |
|---|---|---|---|---|---|---|---|---|---|---|---|
| t = 1 |   | .188<br>8.54 | .178<br>7.53 | .403<br>28.12 | .554<br>64.21 | .576<br>71.99 | .140<br>2.72 | .084<br>.38 | 241 | 3.1 | 2.1 |
| β = 2 | 235 |   | −.048<br>1.36 | .224<br>7.66 | .216<br>7.10 | .221<br>7.45 | −.028<br>.11 | −.118<br>.72 | 598 | 69.8 | 10.5 |
| α = 3 | 232 | 590 |   | .216<br>7.19 | .130<br>2.53 | .161<br>3.91 | −.004<br>.02 | −.029<br>.04 | 592 | 6.2 | 4.1 |
| L = 4 | 147 | 147 | 149 |   | .615<br>167.89 | .582<br>141.37 | −.099<br>2.47 | −.246<br>7.67 | 278 | 43.6 | 16.3 |
| W = 5 | 147 | 147 | 149 | 278 |   | .651<br>203.00 | −.062<br>.96 | −.150<br>2.74 | 278 | 31.5 | 11.0 |
| T = 6 | 147 | 147 | 149 | 278 | 278 |   | .154<br>6.10 | .061<br>.45 | 279 | 8.0 | 3.4 |
| δL = 7 | 138 | 147 | 149 | 252 | 252 | 253 |   | .234<br>6.02 | 268 | 48.7 | 12.6 |
| δD = 8 | 55 | 53 | 55 | 121 | 121 | 122 | 106 |   | 122 | 64.7 | 11.0 |

☐ p = .001

[ ] p = .01

## TABLE 11

### Correlations between Variables: Horner

|  | 1 | 2 | 3 | 4 | 5 | 6 | 7 | 8 | N | $\bar{X}$ | d |
|---|---|---|---|---|---|---|---|---|---|---|---|
| t = 1 |  | .236<br>2.12 | −.234<br>2.09 | .259<br>2.66 | [.413<br>7.61] | .345<br>4.99 | .316<br>3.55 | .520<br>4.82 | 39 | 3.5 | 2.3 |
| β = 2 | 38 |  | −.227<br>3.48 | .020<br>.01 | .182<br>1.23 | .256<br>2.52 | .007<br>.02 | .097<br>.11 | 66 | 66.7 | 10.2 |
| α = 3 | 38 | 66 |  | .144<br>.76 | .010<br>.04 | .127<br>.59 | −.053<br>.09 | −.390<br>2.15 | 63 | 5.5 | 2.7 |
| L = 4 | 39 | 38 | 38 |  | .609<br>52.47 | .520<br>32.98 | −.114<br>1.05 | −.254<br>3.03 | 91 | 33.8 | 14.0 |
| W = 5 | 39 | 38 | 38 | 91 |  | .654<br>66.52 | −.067<br>.36 | −.122<br>.66 | 91 | 26.4 | 8.4 |
| T = 6 | 39 | 38 | 38 | 91 | 91 |  | .211<br>3.73 | .173<br>1.36 | 91 | 6.8 | 2.6 |
| δL = 7 | 34 | 34 | 34 | 82 | 82 | 82 |  | .579<br>19.16 | 82 | 45.0 | 11.9 |
| δD = 8 | 15 | 14 | 14 | 46 | 46 | 46 | 40 |  | 46 | 54.8 | 13.0 |

☐ p = .001

[ ] p = .01

## TABLE 12

### Correlations between Variables: Levi

|  | 1 | 2 | 3 | 4 | 5 | 6 | 7 | 8 | N | $\bar{X}$ | d |
|---|---|---|---|---|---|---|---|---|---|---|---|
| t = 1 |  | .147<br>.79 | −.196<br>1.44 | .315<br>3.97 | .233<br>2.07 | .545<br>15.21 | .273<br>2.74 | −.193<br>.50 | 38 | 6.9 | 3.0 |
| β = 2 | 38 |  | −.002<br>.04 | .107<br>.42 | .336<br>4.58 | .091<br>.30 | −.171<br>1.02 | .217<br>.64 | 108 | 68.8 | 9.9 |
| ∝ = 3 | 38 | 108 |  | .222<br>1.87 | −.175<br>1.14 | −.170<br>1.07 | −.093<br>.30 | −.190<br>.49 | 108 | 6.4 | 4.8 |
| L = 4 | 38 | 38 | 38 |  | .392<br>12.35 | .439<br>16.23 | .226<br>3.55 | .316<br>3.22 | 70 | 55.0 | 17.2 |
| W = 5 | 38 | 38 | 38 | 70 |  | .402<br>13.11 | .425<br>14.55 | .017<br>.09 | 70 | 42.6 | 13.2 |
| T = 6 | 38 | 38 | 38 | 70 | 70 |  | .559<br>29.99 | .283<br>2.53 | 70 | 12.7 | 6.2 |
| δL = 7 | 36 | 36 | 36 | 68 | 68 | 68 |  | .424<br>5.92 | 68 | 54.6 | 13.8 |
| δD = 8 | 15 | 15 | 15 | 31 | 31 | 31 | 29 |  | 31 | 66.6 | 11.4 |

☐ p = .001

[ ] p = .01

## TABLE 13

### Correlations between Variables: Williamson

|   | 1 | 2 | 3 | 4 | 5 | 6 | 7 | 8 | N | $\bar{X}$ | d |
|---|---|---|---|---|---|---|---|---|---|---|---|
| t = 1 |  | .423<br>7.19 | −.120<br>.48 | [ .500<br>11.00 ] | [ .633<br>22.06 ] | .596<br>18.18 | .200<br>1.13 | .119<br>.23 | 35 | 4.4 | 2.5 |
| β = 2 | 35 |  | −.059<br>.53 | .205<br>6.58 | [ .216<br>7.34 ] | [ .225<br>7.99 ] | .078<br>.18 | .341<br>2.37 | 153 | 72.0 | 11.1 |
| α = 3 | 35 | 153 |  | .014<br>.03 | −.147<br>3.31 | −.030<br>.14 | −.311<br>3.11 | .535<br>7.22 | 153 | 6.6 | 4.6 |
| L = 4 | 35 | 152 | 152 |  | .602<br>101.75 | .633<br>119.68 | .119<br>.78 | .282<br>3.20 | 181 | 41.2 | 15.2 |
| W = 5 | 35 | 152 | 152 | 181 |  | .684<br>157.38 | .331<br>6.64 | .329<br>4.49 | 181 | 30.3 | 10.9 |
| T = 6 | 35 | 152 | 152 | 181 | 181 |  | [ .352<br>7.64 ] | [ .494<br>11.94 ] | 181 | 8.9 | 4.4 |
| δL = 7 | 29 | 31 | 31 | 56 | 56 | 56 |  | .390<br>5.38 | 56 | 58.2 | 10.3 |
| δD = 8 | 18 | 20 | 20 | 39 | 39 | 39 | 32 |  | 39 | 67.7 | 7.9 |

☐ p = .001
[ ] p = .01

## TABLE 14

### Correlations between Variables: Quad

|   | 1 | 2 | 3 | 4 | 5 | 6 | 7 | 8 | N | $\bar{X}$ | d |
|---|---|---|---|---|---|---|---|---|---|---|---|
| t = 1 |   | .249<br>22.08 | .003<br>.03 | .069<br>1.60 | .380<br>56.54 | .309<br>35.36 | .134<br>2.50 | .117<br>.33 | 337 | 4.3 | 2.4 |
| β = 2 | 336 |   | .053<br>.93 | .015<br>.08 | .115<br>4.48 | .257<br>23.62 | .353<br>19.35 | .159<br>.62 | 336 | 73.2 | 11.9 |
| ∝ = 3 | 334 | 334 |   | .087<br>2.54 | −.077<br>1.99 | −.039<br>.51 | .115<br>1.81 | .115<br>.32 | 335 | 7.8 | 6.8 |
| L = 4 | 337 | 336 | 335 |   | .175<br>13.96 | .386<br>77.39 | .088<br>1.88 | −.345<br>8.24 | 445 | 49.1 | 13.7 |
| W = 5 | 337 | 336 | 335 | 445 |   | .367<br>68.80 | .062<br>.93 | −.065<br>.26 | 445 | 31.1 | 9.5 |
| T = 6 | 337 | 336 | 335 | 445 | 445 |   | .375<br>39.44 | −.024<br>.04 | 445 | 8.6 | 3.3 |
| $\delta_L$ = 7 | 139 | 138 | 137 | 243 | 243 | 243 |   | .213<br>2.76 | 243 | 47.4 | 11.3 |
| $\delta_D$ = 8 | 26 | 26 | 26 | 63 | 63 | 63 | 60 |   | 63 | 66.0 | 10.2 |

☐ p = .001

[ ] p = .01

## TABLE 15

### Correlations between Variables: Vernon

|        | 1  | 2           | 3             | 4              | 5               | 6                | 7               | 8             | N   | $\bar{X}$ | d    |
|--------|----|-------------|---------------|----------------|-----------------|------------------|-----------------|---------------|-----|-----------|------|
| t = 1  |    | .004<br>.01 | .058<br>.79   | .282<br>7.60   | .509<br>30.77   | .471<br>25.09    | .300<br>4.25    | .040<br>.02   | 90  | 3.5       | 2.2  |
| β = 2  | 88 |             | −.168<br>4.44 | .009<br>.01    | −.022<br>.07    | .062<br>.59      | .285<br>3.80    | .010<br>.01   | 155 | 72.6      | 10.8 |
| ∝ = 3  | 89 | 155         |               | .116<br>2.09   | .024<br>.09     | .051<br>.39      | .060<br>.16     | −.031<br>.01  | 156 | 5.5       | 4.5  |
| L = 4  | 90 | 154         | 155           |                | .692<br>178.26  | .816<br>386.59   | .302<br>7.93    | .205<br>1.49  | 196 | 29.0      | 13.9 |
| W = 5  | 90 | 154         | 155           | 196            |                 | .791<br>324.27   | .400<br>15.05   | .193<br>1.31  | 196 | 23.8      | 9.8  |
| T = 6  | 90 | 154         | 155           | 196            | 196             |                  | .430<br>17.92   | .364<br>5.19  | 196 | 7.0       | 4.7  |
| δL = 7 | 45 | 45          | 45            | 81             | 81              | 81               |                 | .442<br>6.80  | 81  | 51.2      | 11.4 |
| δD = 8 | 15 | 15          | 15            | 36             | 36              | 36               | 30              |               | 36  | 59.7      | 13.2 |

▢ p = .001

[ ] p = .01

quantitative scale (simple measurements of length in millimeters or of angles in degrees). Striking platform lateral lengths (w) were not obtained from the Quad sample. This variable was, therefore, not considered in the correlation.

The matrices present several values for each pair of correlates. The left half of each matrix indicates the number of cases (n) correlated for each pair of variables. In the right half of each matrix are entered two sets of values for each pair of variables. The upper entry for each pair is the product-moment correlation coefficient (r) for that pair. This value is obtained from the formula:

$$r = \frac{n \Sigma XY - \Sigma X \Sigma Y}{\sqrt{[n \Sigma X^2 - (\Sigma X)^2][n \Sigma Y^2 - (\Sigma Y)^2]}}$$

In this formula, n is the number of pairs, X is a value for one of a pair of variables, and Y is a value for the other variable in the pair. Immediately below each r value is entered the significance score (F) for that r. Values of F are obtained from the formula:

$$F_{1,n-2} = \frac{r^2}{1-r^2}(n-2).$$

Those values of F which are significant at the .001 level are boxed and those which are significant at the .01 level are enclosed in brackets. Significance at the .001 level means that there is only 1 chance in 1000 that, for a stated value of n, a value of F of the magnitude being tested will occur by chance. Significance at the .01 level indicates that a given F score could be expected by chance alone in 1 of every 100 cases. The hypothesis being tested is that the observed correlations do not differ from randomness. Significance limits have been set at the .01 level. F scores which meet or exceed these limits are here considered to indicate that this hypothesis may be rejected and that true, non-random relationships exist between the variables being tested.

In addition to the correlation matrices, each table lists the total number of cases (N), the mean value ($\bar{X}$), and the standard deviation (d) of each variable. It should be remembered that these correlations apply to total sample sets only. Correlations of the same variables restricted to tools or to utilized flakes would probably display variations from the results obtained for these total sample sets.

A number of consistent correlations appear in the matrices. Length, width, and thickness of artifacts are positively correlated in the pooled data and in every sample. These correlations are uniformly high and unvarying; as one of these dimensions increases, the other two tend also to increase. A somewhat less pronounced but still high correlation exists between striking platform thickness (t) and artifact width and thickness; W and T tend to increase in size when t becomes larger. The correlation between t and T is not apparent in the Horner sample but this may be a product of the small number of cases in the sample. It should be noted that $F_{txT}$ is significant at the .05 level in the Horner sample. (In general, it would seem that small sample size is depressing the significance score in both the Horner and Levi samples.) $F_{txW}$—in fact all correlations involving t—for the Levi sample have been influenced by the truncated recording procedure used for this variable; therefore, significant correlations between t and other variables will not necessarily become obvious in this sample.

Several other significant correlations appear in the pooled data and in three or more of the site samples. The most consistent of these are T x $\beta$ and T x $\delta_L$. These are both strong correlations and indicate that, in general, thickness tends to increase as the flake angle approaches 90° and that the steepness of lateral retouch tends to increase as specimen thickness increases. A relationship between width (W) and $< \beta$ and $< \delta_L$ also tends to exist but this is not so strong or so persistent. Other slightly noted and irregular tendencies are those of $<\delta_D$ to increase with increases in $<\beta_L$ and T for $<\alpha$ to increase with increases in length (L).

Only one case of negative correlation appears in the tables. In the Lindenmeier and Quad samples, artifact length varies inversely with the distal retouch angle—as L decreases in value, $< \delta_D$ increases. This tendency is also apparent (.05 level of significance) in the Horner sample.

In addition to the above instances of mutual covariation, it will be useful to list those variable sets which appear to be largely unaffected by variation in other variables. There are two main components in this group. The most independently variable element among the eight variables under consideration is $< \alpha$ which seems to be unaffected by variation in all other factors except artifact length. There is, however, a slight tendency to mutual covariation between $<\alpha$ and t in the Lindenmeier sample. The second set of largely independent variables consists of $<\delta_L$ and $<\delta_D$. Notice that $<\delta_L$ is unaffected by variations in artifact length, striking platform thickness, and artifact axis orientation and that $<\delta_D$ is unaffected by all variables other than artifact thickness, lateral retouch and, to some extent, artifact length. It would appear, therefore, that the retouch angles are positively related to each other and to artifact thickness and width but that they are essentially independent of other variables except that $<\delta_D$ tends to be negatively correlated with artifact length.

## Comparisons between Samples

Tables 16 - 23 present *t* scores of the differences between mean values ($\bar{X}$) of each quantitative variable obtained for each sample tested against the analogous value for every other sample. These tables are organized in matrix form in order to indicate clearly the relationships within each variable set that exist among all the samples. Those variables omitted in the previous set of tables are also omitted here. The *t* scores were derived from the formula:

$$t = \frac{\bar{X}_1 - \bar{X}_2}{e_1 - e_2}.$$

Significance levels are set at the .05 level. Those scores which are significant at this level are boxed. The tables also indicate the number of values (N) for and the mean value ($\bar{X}$) of each variable obtained from each sample.

Table 16 indicates that the striking platform thickness (t) in the Levi sample is signifcantly greater than it is in any other sample. The Quad sample also shows some tendency to greater platform size but this dimension is not so great in this sample as it is in the Levi sample. The Williamson sample, with the second largest absolute value of t, does not appear to be significantly different in this variable from any other sample. This reinforces the observation that Levi specimens have larger platforms than do those from the other samples.

Table 17 indicates that the differences, noted earlier in this description, between the values of $<\beta$ obtained for the Lindenmeier-Blackwater-Horner-Levi group of sites and the Shoop-Williamson-Quad-Vernon group are real. The mean value of this variable in the latter group is, collectively and individually, significantly larger than it is in the former group. The only deviation from this general pattern occurs in the tool subcategory in which the Vernon sample does not differ from the Lindenmeier-Blackwater-Horner-Levi group ($t_{Lind-Vern}$ = 0.53) but does differ from Quad (t = 2.52) and Shoop. Artifacts in the Quad sample tend to have significantly higher values of $<\alpha$ than do those in the other samples. As shown by Table 18, the differences among the other samples are not significant. Quad tools are also significantly more oblique than are tools at Lindenmeier (t = 2.00) but Quad tools do not differ in this respect from Shoop, Williamson, Levi, and Vernon tools. Those tables (19, 20, and 21) which present comparisons of dimensional data document a considerable variation in length, width, and thickness among the samples. All Levi artifacts are significantly longer, wider, and thicker than are all others. Quad artifacts, as a group, are longer than those from other samples except Levi but they fall in the middle range of width and thickness; Quad tools maintain these positions. There is no significant difference in artifact size between the Lindenmeier, Blackwater, and Williamson samples except that Blackwater specimens are significantly thinner than the others. Williamson tools (in contrast to all Williamson specimens taken together) are thick ($t_{Lind-Will}$ = 2.36, $t_{Levi-Will}$ = 1.00). The Horner and Shoop samples display consistently smaller values for all dimensions than do all others. Although specimen size in the Vernon sample is generally small, Vernon tool size is significantly larger than that observed in most other samples ($t_L$ Vern-Quad = 0.68, $t_W$ Vern-Lind = 2.33, $t_T$ Vern-Quad = 3.46).

Tables 22 and 23 indicate that retouch angles on Levi, Shoop, and Williamson specimens are significantly steeper than are those on other specimens. Quad distal angles are also in this category. Retouch angles on Horner specimens are significantly more acute than are those found on specimens in the other collections.

## Tool Categories

The foregoing presentation focuses on total assemblage characteristics and is intended to be a full descriptive statement of the aggregate sample data. It should be useful, however, to consider the different tool forms which may be recognized in the samples

## TABLE 16
### Between Sample Comparisons of $t$

|  | | 1 | 2 | 3 | 4 | 5 | 6 | 7 | 8 | N | $\bar{X}$ |
|---|---|---|---|---|---|---|---|---|---|---|---|
| Lindenmeier | : 1 | — | — | 0.57 | 4.77 | — | 1.85 | 2.26 | 0.61 | 597 | 3.13 |
| Blackwater | : 2 | | — | — | — | — | — | — | — | — | — |
| Horner | : 3 | | | | 3.61 | — | 1.03 | 1.06 | 0.04 | 66 | 3.53 |
| Levi | : 4 | | | | | — | 2.55 | 3.30 | 3.96 | 108 | 6.88 |
| Shoop | : 5 | | | | | | — | — | — | — | — |
| Williamson | : 6 | | | | | | | 0.22 | 1.15 | 153 | 4.44 |
| Quad | : 7 | | | | | | | | 1.29 | 336 | 4.28 |
| Vernon | : 8 | | | | | | | | | 157 | 3.50 |

☐ $p = .05$

## TABLE 17
### Between Sample Comparisons of $\leq \beta$

|  | | 1 | 2 | 3 | 4 | 5 | 6 | 7 | 8 | N | $\bar{X}$ |
|---|---|---|---|---|---|---|---|---|---|---|---|
| Lindenmeier | : 1 | | 1.47 | 1.54 | 0.94 | 3.41 | 2.61 | 3.87 | 2.65 | 597 | 69.9 |
| Blackwater | : 2 | | | 0.07 | 1.30 | 3.88 | 3.39 | 4.43 | 3.82 | 64 | 66.8 |
| Horner | : 3 | | | | 1.41 | 4.09 | 3.60 | 4.69 | 4.04 | 66 | 66.7 |
| Levi | : 4 | | | | | 2.89 | 2.35 | 3.47 | 2.81 | 108 | 68.8 |
| Shoop | : 5 | | | | | | 0.59 | 0.32 | 0.15 | 160 | 72.8 |
| Williamson | : 6 | | | | | | | 0.97 | 0.45 | 153 | 72.0 |
| Quad | : 7 | | | | | | | | 0.49 | 336 | 73.2 |
| Verson | : 8 | | | | | | | | | 157 | 72.6 |

☐ $p = .05$

## TABLE 18
### Between Sample Comparisons of $<\alpha$

|  | 1 | 2 | 3 | 4 | 5 | 6 | 7 | 8 | N | $\bar{X}$ |
|---|---|---|---|---|---|---|---|---|---|---|
| Lindenmeier : 1 |  | 0.12 | 1.16 | 0.38 | 0.39 | 0.82 | [2.43] | 0.14 | 592 | 6.6 |
| Blackwater : 2 |  |  | 0.76 | 0.40 | 0.21 | 0.74 | [1.98] | 0.01 | 62 | 6.5 |
| Horner : 3 |  |  |  | 1.26 | 0.59 | 1.71 | [3.13] | 0.86 | 66 | 5.8 |
| Levi : 4 |  |  |  |  | 0.64 | 0.34 | 1.65 | 0.44 | 108 | 6.9 |
| Shoop : 5 |  |  |  |  |  | 1.02 | [2.35] | 0.23 | 95 | 6.3 |
| Williamson : 6 |  |  |  |  |  |  | 1.40 | 0.83 | 153 | 7.2 |
| Quad : 7 |  |  |  |  |  |  |  | [2.33] | 335 | 8.4 |
| Vernon : 8 |  |  |  |  |  |  |  |  | 156 | 6.5 |

☐ $p = .05$

## TABLE 19
### Between Sample Comparisons of L

|  | 1 | 2 | 3 | 4 | 5 | 6 | 7 | 8 | N | $\bar{X}$ |
|---|---|---|---|---|---|---|---|---|---|---|
| Lindenmeier : 1 |  | 0.60 | [6.39] | [6.30] | [12.03] | 1.64 | [3.92] | [10.69] | 578 | 43.6 |
| Blackwater : 2 |  |  | [6.12] | [5.11] | [10.65] | 1.28 | [2.58] | [5.12] | 118 | 44.6 |
| Horner : 3 |  |  |  | [11.16] | 3.99 | [4.33] | [10.30] | [3.19] | 91 | 33.8 |
| Levi : 4 |  |  |  |  | [15.97] | [7.81] | [3.64] | [14.86] | 70 | 55.1 |
| Shoop : 5 |  |  |  |  |  | [9.36] | [17.50] | 0.75 | 132 | 28.4 |
| Williamson : 6 |  |  |  |  |  |  | [5.98] | [8.22] | 181 | 41.2 |
| Quad : 7 |  |  |  |  |  |  |  | [15.62] | 444 | 49.1 |
| Vernon : 8 |  |  |  |  |  |  |  |  | 196 | 29.0 |

☐ $p = .05$

## TABLE 20
### Between Sample Comparisons of W

|  | 1 | 2 | 3 | 4 | 5 | 6 | 7 | 8 | N | $\bar{X}$ |
|---|---|---|---|---|---|---|---|---|---|---|
| Lindenmeier : 1 |  |  |  |  |  |  |  |  | 578 | 31.5 |
| Blackwater : 2 |  | 1.76 |  |  |  |  |  |  | 118 | 29.2 |
| Horner : 3 |  |  | 4.83 |  |  |  |  |  | 91 | 26.4 |
| Levi : 4 |  |  | 1.92 | 7.33 |  |  |  |  | 70 | 42.6 |
| Shoop : 5 |  |  |  | 8.47 | 9.17 |  |  |  | 132 | 21.5 |
| Williamson : 6 |  |  |  | 10.82 | 5.42 | 1.65 |  |  | 181 | 30.3 |
| Quad : 7 |  |  |  |  | 3.37 | 0.72 | 0.95 |  | 444 | 31.1 |
| Vernon : 8 |  |  |  |  | 14.42 | 3.08 | 1.59 | 6.86 | 196 | 23.9 |
|  |  |  |  |  |  | 8.39 | 4.34 | 3.69 |  |  |
|  |  |  |  |  |  | 6.91 | 8.40 | 1.59 |  |  |
|  |  |  |  |  |  |  | 9.09 | 12.56 |  |  |
|  |  |  |  |  |  |  | 0.89 | 1.80 |  |  |
|  |  |  |  |  |  |  |  | 4.88 |  |  |
|  |  |  |  |  |  |  |  | 6.53 |  |  |

☐ p = .05

## TABLE 21
### Between Sample Comparisons of T

|  | 1 | 2 | 3 | 4 | 5 | 6 | 7 | 8 | N | $\bar{X}$ |
|---|---|---|---|---|---|---|---|---|---|---|
| Lindenmeier : 1 |  |  |  |  |  |  |  |  | 578 | 8.0 |
| Blackwater : 2 |  | 2.78 |  |  |  |  |  |  | 118 | 5.9 |
| Horner : 3 |  |  | 1.73 |  |  |  |  |  | 91 | 6.8 |
| Levi : 4 |  |  | 1.13 | 4.90 |  |  |  |  | 70 | 12.8 |
| Shoop : 5 |  |  |  | 6.55 | 1.85 |  |  |  | 132 | 6.8 |
| Williamson : 6 |  |  |  | 5.94 | 1.19 | 1.22 |  |  | 181 | 8.9 |
| Quad : 7 |  |  |  |  | 0.00 | 3.61 | 0.98 |  | 444 | 8.6 |
| Vernon : 8 |  |  |  |  | 6.12 | 2.71 | 3.74 | 1.35 | 196 | 7.0 |
|  |  |  |  |  |  | 3.75 | 2.74 | 1.32 |  |  |
|  |  |  |  |  |  | 2.86 | 4.40 | 0.26 |  |  |
|  |  |  |  |  |  |  | 2.96 | 5.56 |  |  |
|  |  |  |  |  |  |  | 0.43 | 0.27 |  |  |
|  |  |  |  |  |  |  |  | 2.32 |  |  |
|  |  |  |  |  |  |  |  | 2.26 |  |  |

☐ p = .05

## TABLE 22
### Between Sample Comparisons of $<\delta_L$

|  | 1 | 2 | 3 | 4 | 5 | 6 | 7 | 8 | N | $\bar{X}$ |
|---|---|---|---|---|---|---|---|---|---|---|
| Lindenmeier : 1 |  | 0.00 | 2.08 | 3.83 | 2.89 | 6.12 | 1.63 | 1.40 | 267 | 48.7 |
| Blackwater : 2 |  |  | 1.66 | 3.16 | 2.45 | 4.94 | 1.23 | 1.12 | 39 | 48.5 |
| Horner : 3 |  |  |  | 5.20 | 4.23 | 7.29 | 0.70 | 3.10 | 82 | 45.0 |
| Levi : 4 |  |  |  |  | 0.50 | 1.71 | 5.15 | 2.32 | 68 | 54.6 |
| Shoop : 5 |  |  |  |  |  | 2.10 | 4.05 | 1.60 | 139 | 53.9 |
| Williamson : 6 |  |  |  |  |  |  | 7.55 | 4.28 | 58 | 58.2 |
| Quad : 7 |  |  |  |  |  |  |  | 2.82 | 244 | 47.4 |
| Vernon : 8 |  |  |  |  |  |  |  |  | 81 | 51.2 |

☐ $p = .05$

## TABLE 23
### Between Sample Comparisons of $<\delta_D$

|  | 1 | 2 | 3 | 4 | 5 | 6 | 7 | 8 | N | $\bar{X}$ |
|---|---|---|---|---|---|---|---|---|---|---|
| Lindenmeier : 1 |  | — | 5.83 | 0.60 | 0.00 | 1.99 | 0.66 | 2.78 | 122 | 64.7 |
| Blackwater : 2 |  |  | — | — | — | — | — | — | — | — |
| Horner : 3 |  |  |  | 5.49 | 6.01 | 7.24 | 6.11 | 2.45 | 46 | 54.8 |
| Levi : 4 |  |  |  |  | 0.59 | 1.09 | 0.00 | 2.89 | 31 | 66.6 |
| Shoop : 5 |  |  |  |  |  | 1.80 | 0.69 | 2.86 | 132 | 65.1 |
| Williamson : 6 |  |  |  |  |  |  | 1.25 | 4.27 | 38 | 67.7 |
| Quad : 7 |  |  |  |  |  |  |  | 3.19 | 57 | 66.0 |
| Vernon : 8 |  |  |  |  |  |  |  |  | 36 | 59.7 |

☐ $p = .05$

separately, as entities in themselves. Such a consideration is still descriptive but it concentrates on those overlapping formal variables whose systematic co-occurrence on the same artifacts can be demonstrated. It also provides a framework within which tool variation may be inventoried. In the description of tool forms which follows, scaled data which define the formal characteristics of specimens are utilized. These data were obtained for tools but not for unmodified flakes whether these latter were utilized or not. Only whole tools or those with but minor fragments missing are considered.

In a systematic descriptive procedure, the generalities of formal variation of tool morphology are of primary interest and the facts of individual tool configuration are subsumed within the general descriptive structure. The individual facts are not ignored. On the contrary, they provide the very basis upon which general categories are established and set limits to the range of formal variation included within each category. Anyone who has worked with collections of stone tools will agree with Sackett (1966: 357) when he says that attributes "almost always exhibit a degree of seemingly random combinations." The question is, how to deal with this variation. It is not merely a matter of lumping or splitting attributes and artifacts into larger or smaller segmental units. If one is interested solely in cataloguing all of the varieties of shapes which have been imposed upon raw stone, splitting is presumably a perfectly logical procedure. But the underlying structure of artifact variation will remain hidden.

Anthropologically-motivated archaeologists will not be satisfied with such procedures. They will want to discover the cultural processes that were operating in the production and utilization of artifact populations. And the elucidation of cultural processes depends upon the recognition of those common elements that underlie individual variations in form and meaning. A comprehensive formal presentation that recognizes regularity in artifact variation may lead to inferences concerning the sociocultural processes associated with those artifacts while a mere recounting of facts satisfies only itself.

Figures 25 - 29 present the 13 formal tool categories that were identified in the samples. It should be emphasized that these categories were defined from the data recorded on punch-cards and not directly from the artifacts themselves. No prior sorting of the specimens into tool types was attempted. The artifacts could not have been directly compared and sorted even if it had been desirable to do so, since no more than two sample sets were ever present in the same place at the same time. The categories are useful, therefore, not only in themselves but also in that they provide graphic demonstration of a method for comparing specimen groups which are not concurrently available.

Each category is defined by a set of attribute values which co-occur on a large number of individual specimens. The attribute clusters were arrived at by a sorting process in which one attribute was paired with another until all cases of co-occurrence had been isolated. The resultant pairs were then correlated with a third attribute, and so forth until all attributes had been treated. The first sorting produced 28 sets of attribute clusters and 16 isolated clusters. These 28 groupings were subjected to a second sorting in which adjacent clusters differing in only one attribute were combined. For example, the clusters 4 - 2.121 and 4 - 3.121 differ only in their representation of proximal edge contours on different specimens. They are, therefore, combined and considered to be variants of one category and this intracategory variation is noted in the category descriptive code. Twelve of the formal categories presented in Figures 25 - 29 are the product of this second sorting. The first five categories correspond to the class of artifacts generally referred to as "endscrapers" and the last seven to "sidescrapers" and "knives." The 16 isolated clusters were found to possess two traits in common; (1) thinness and (2) small worked tips but no other retouch. They were, therefore, combined into one heterogeneous category (Category VI) of graver tips.

A number of weaknesses are inherent in this procedure. The most serious of these is the lack of a suitable method for testing the significance of the associations implicit in the categories. It is true that a non-parametric technique (partialing) for cross-tabulating data of this kind is available. (A well reasoned paper by Sackett [1966] in which partialing was employed offered suggestive but inconclusive results.) But the labor involved in these calculations, given the number of variables under consideration, is enormous. Furthermore, such tests are extremely sensitive to sampling error control and sample size. Sampling error is potentially great in all of the samples under consideration and sample size is very small in some cases. In view of these facts, significance tests were not thought to be applicable in this case.

It must be stressed, however, that these categories are not meant to represent artifact types; they are merely descriptive devices which should be useful in comparing the formal tool configurations found in a number of sites. Moreover, as more work of a formal nature is carried out on stone tool assemblages and more precise techniques are developed for describing these assemblages, the descriptive categories presented here will be modified or replaced by more useful formulations.

The descriptive codes assigned to each formal category are listed below. These codes are composed of four sets of entries each of which is separated from the others by a colon. Summary data of dimensions as well as of the flake angle and medial axis characteristic of the category is appended to the code. The first entry set describes the shape characteristic of the category. The first digit of this set refers to maximum width position; the next four digits refer respectively to proximal, left lateral, distal, and right lateral edge contour; the final letter refers to longitudinal section outline. The extent of intracategory variation is noted in the following manner: $\frac{2}{3}$. The second entry set designates the values of edge angles as follows: lateral angle/distal angle. Values in parentheses are alternate variations and indicate bimodal distributions of values for the appropriate variable. The third entry set designates retouch position. Parentheses indicate that retouch may or may not occur on a particular edge of individual specimens within a category. The final entry indicates the percentage of incidence of tool accessory forms within a category. Mean values and standard deviations are given for dimensions. Flake angle and medial axis values are given as means rounded to the nearest degree. In the drawings, dashed lines indicate shape variations and short, paired lines mark the extent of one standard deviation in size range.

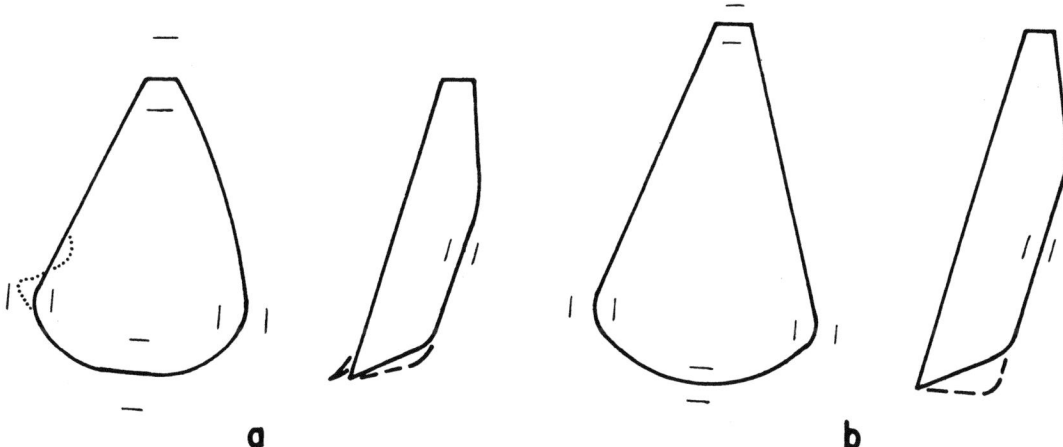

Fig. 25. Formal Categories I - IV. *a*, I; *b*, II.

Category I (Fig. 25, *a*)
    4 - 3.322-B : 50°/55° : (L)/D/(L) : 22%
        2     D
        L = 31.4 ± 7.6 mm
        W = 23.8 ± 4.8 mm
        T = 7.3 ± 1.5 mm
        $\beta$ = 73°
        $\alpha$ = 5°

Category II (Fig. 25, *b*).
    5 - 3.313-B : 55°/(55°) (75°) : (L)/D/(L) : O
        2   2D
        L = 37.9 ± 4.5 mm
        W = 24.8 ± 4.7 mm
        T = 8.7 ± 1.5 mm
        $\beta$ = 73°
        $\alpha$ = 5°

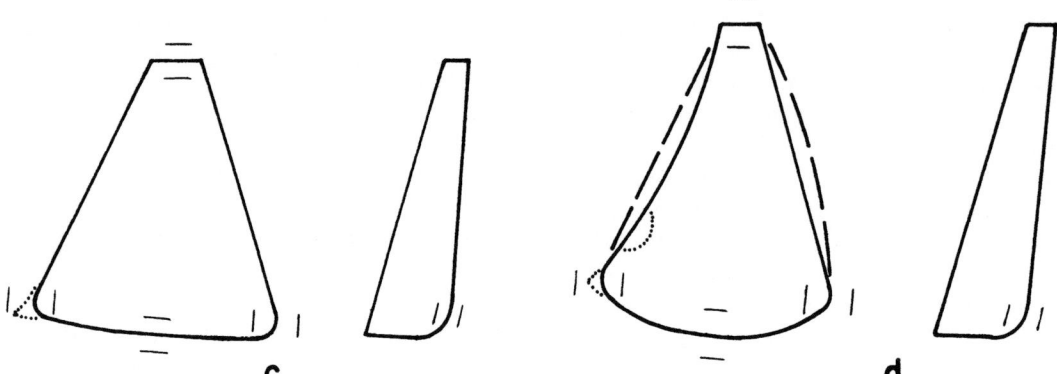

Fig. 25. Formal Categories I - IV. *c*, III; *d*, IV.

Category III (Fig. 25, *c*).
5 - 3.332-C : 60°/75° : (L)/D/(L) : 36%
6 2    B
   L = 28.6 ± 3.7 mm
   W = 25.6 ± 5.1 mm
   T = 8.6 ± 1.5 mm
   $\beta$ = 73°
   $\alpha$ = 5°

Category IV (Fig. 25, *d*).
5 - 3.423-C : 60°/75° : (L)/D/(L) : 42%
2 2    B
   L = 32.6 ± 6.1 mm
   W = 25.0 ± 4.9 mm
   T = 8.6 ± 3.5 mm
   $\beta$ = 73°
   $\alpha$ = 5°

Category V (Fig. 26, *a*).
4 - 2.221-B : 45° - 60°/45° - 60° : L/D/L : 0
5   3 3
   L = 35.2 ± 4.2 mm
   W = 30.4 ± 4.0 mm
   T = 9.5 ± 5.2 mm
   $\beta$ = 73°
   $\alpha$ = 5°

Category VI (Fig. 26, *b*).
2 - 2.266-A : 40° - 50°/40° - 50° : (L)/(D)/(L) : 100%
6   6 403 D
   L = 40.6 ± 7.3 mm
   W = 31.9 ± 6.4 mm
   T = 6.2 ± 2.4 mm
   $\beta$ = 35° - 80°
   $\alpha$ = 2° - 25°

Category VII (Fig. 26, *c*).
  1
2 - 2.206-A : (45°) (65°)/ . . . : L/(D)/ : 10%
  3   1 D
   L = 63.4 ± 11.2 mm
   W = 37.0 ± 8.9 mm
   T = 12.6 ± 5.7 mm
   $\beta$ = 72°
   $\alpha$ = 9°

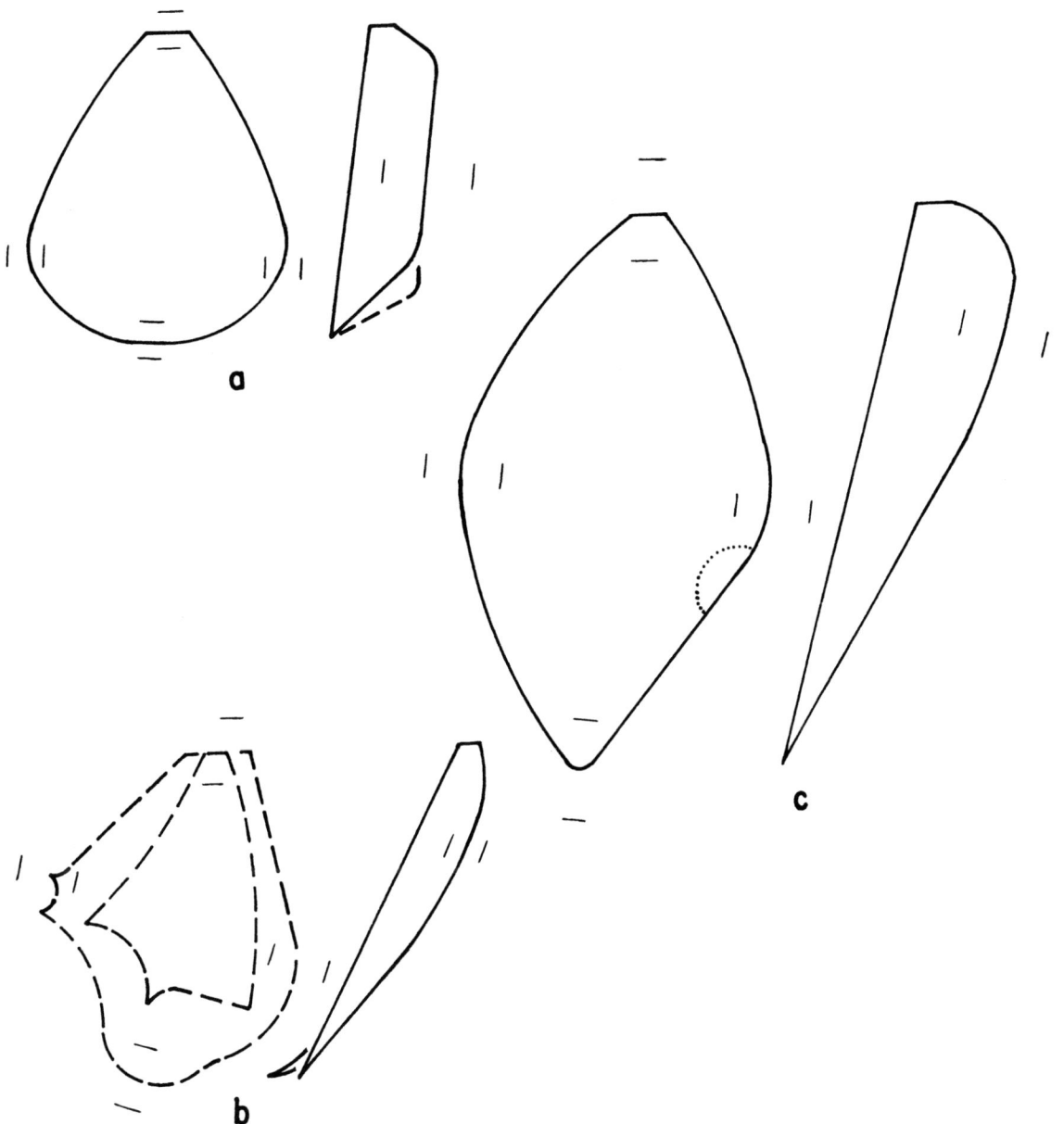

Fig. 26. Formal Categories V - VII. *a*, V; *b*, VI; *c*, VII.

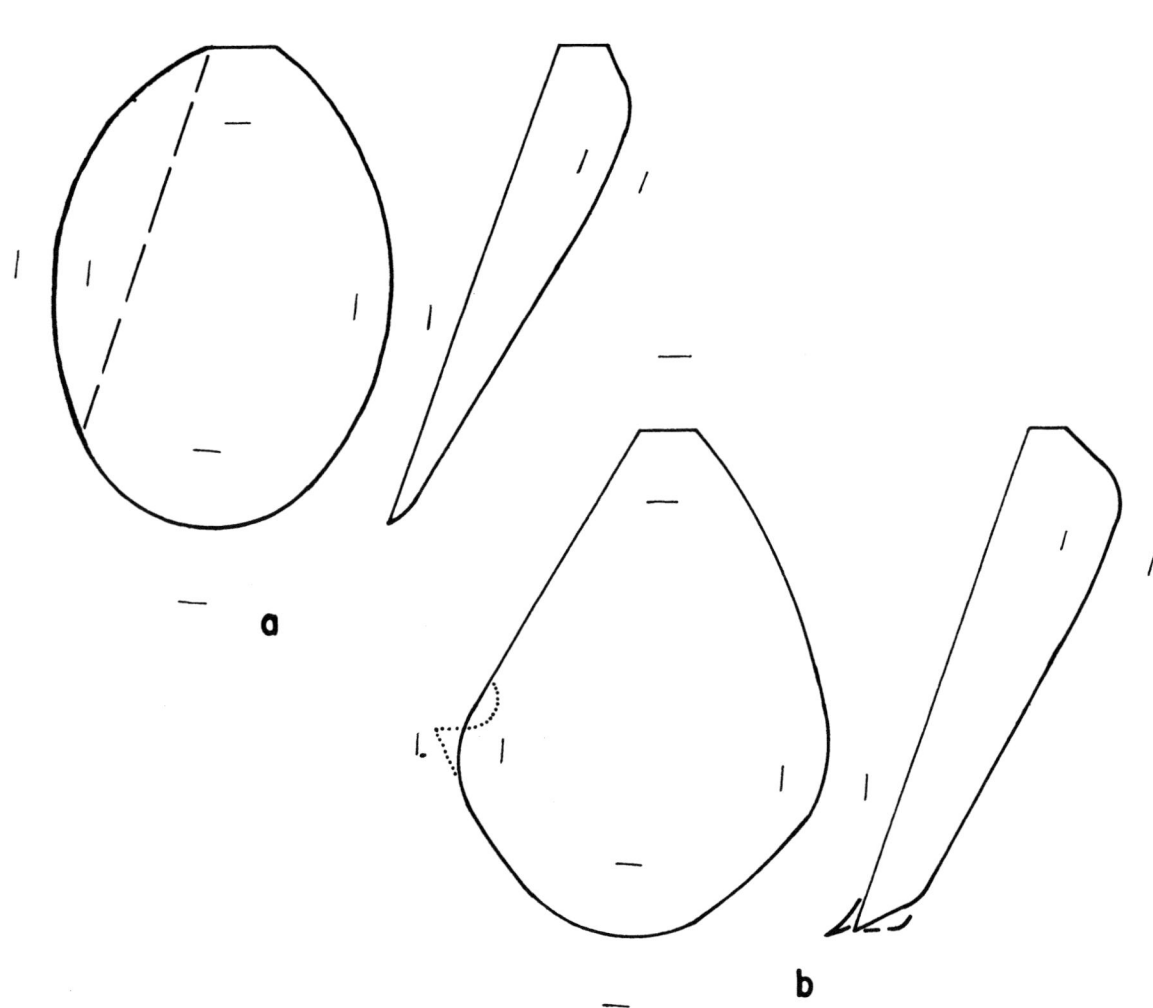

Fig. 27. Formal Categories VIII - IX. *a* VIII; *b*, IX.

Category VIII (Fig. 27, *a*).
   3 - 3.211-A : (30° - 45°) (65°)/ . . . : L/ / (L) : 0
   4   3
     L = 49.9 ± 16.6 mm
     W = 36.9 ± 8.3 mm
     T = 9.6 ± 3.3 mm
     $\beta$ = 69°
     $\alpha$ = 6°

Category IX (Fig. 27, *b*).
   4 - 2.312-A : (45°) (65°)/(45°) (65°) : L/D/L : 30%
   3   21 D
     L = 53.1 ± 14.9 mm
     W = 40.4 ± 9.1 mm
     T = 12.2 ± 5.1 mm
     $\beta$ = 71°
     $\alpha$ = 6°

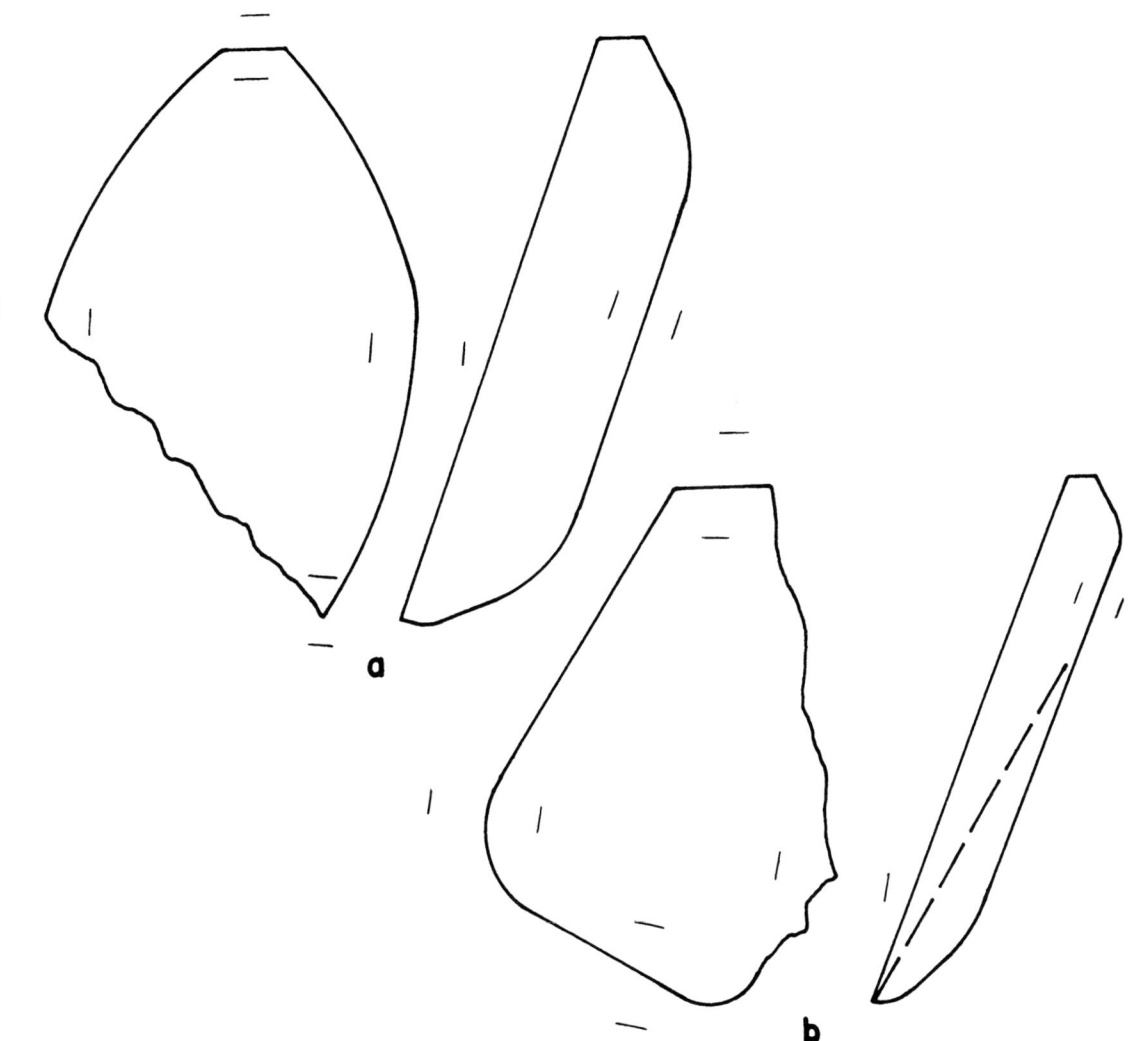

Fig. 28. Formal Categories X - XI. *a*, X; *b*, XI.

Category X (Fig. 28, *a*).
  3 - 3.262-B : 50°/ . . . : L/ /L : 17%
  4  2 3 6
    L = 58.6 ± 6.6 mm
    W = 39.8 ± 10.6 mm
    T = 14.5 ± 3.8 mm
    $\beta$ = 69°
    $\alpha$ = 6°

Category XI (Fig. 28, *b*).
  4 - 3.236-B : 50°/ . . . : L/ / : 10%
  5    1 3 D
    L = 52.1 ± 11.3 mm
    W = 37.9 ± 12.3 mm
    T = 8.8 ± 2.3 mm
    $\beta$ = 67°
    $\alpha$ = 4° - 12°

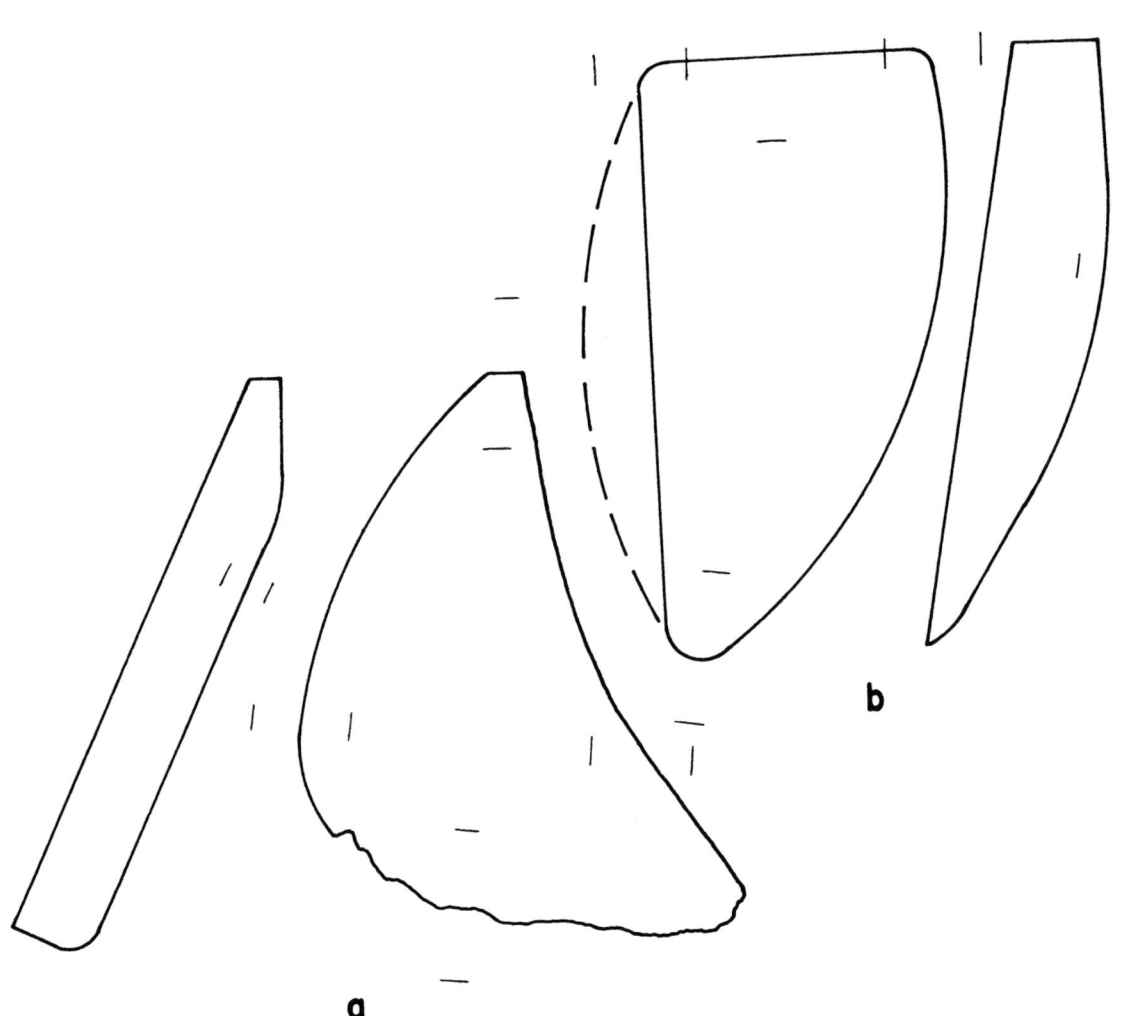

Fig. 29. Formal Categories XII - XIII. *a*, XII; *b*, XIII.

Category XII (Fig. 29, *a*).
    4 - 3.264-B : 50°/ . . . : L// : 0
       5 D
       L = 56.7 ± 15.6 mm
       W = 38.4 ± 11.3 mm
       T = 8.9 ± 2.6 mm
       $\beta$ = 64°
       $\alpha$ = 6°

Category XIII (Fig. 29, *b*).
    0 - 3.312-B : (45°) (70°)/ . . . : L// : 0
      1  2  3
       L = 64.7 ± 16.3 mm
       W = 30.0 ± 8.7 mm
       T = 9.3 ± 2.9 mm
       $\beta$ = 80°
       $\alpha$ = 10°

## Artifact Populations of Sites

As a final step in the description of the data, the co-occurrence in each sample of the formal tool categories, projectile point types, and other artifact forms will be considered. Tables 24 and 25 summarize the frequencies of occurrence of the different artifact forms in each sample. Table 25 also lists the associated faunal and vegetal remains found with the artifacts.

These data suggest that the eight samples may be divided into five groups each of which is characterized by a different tool assemblage. The Lindenmeier and Quad samples are characterized by a relatively broad spectrum of tool types with a wide range of edge angle values. Both the Lindenmeier and the Quad sites have produced large numbers of finished projectile points as well as points in various stages of manufacture. Bifaces constitute somewhat more than 10 per cent of these samples. Cores are present but are not numerous and the ratio of debitage to completed tools is low. No food-grinding stones have been reported from either site.

The Blackwater sample is composed primarily of tools with retouch on one lateral edge only or with retouch on lateral and distal edges. Lateral edge retouch tends to be acute and distal retouch, when it occurs, is normally nothing more than a continuation of lateral retouch. Endscrapers are all but nonexistent in this sample. The Blackwater site has yielded finished Clovis points but no preforms or incomplete points. Bifaces but not cores are included in the assemblage. The debitage:tool ratio is very low.

All of the statements made about the Blackwater assemblage apply equally to the Horner materials except that the latter include a relatively large proportion of endscrapers with low distal retouch angles. Eden and Scottsbluff points rather than fluted forms are present in the Horner collection. There are no preforms.

The Levi and Vernon samples are dominated by tools which are retouched on both lateral edges or on lateral and distal edges. There are no endscrapers in the Levi collection and only one in that from Vernon. Retouch is steep on Levi specimens but only moderately steep on those from Vernon. Specimens in both samples are characterized by a high proportion of accessory tips and concavities. Food-grinding stones occur in both collections as do preforms and bifaces. Cores are numerous and the debitage:tool ratio is high in both assemblages.

The most frequent tool form in the Shoop and Williamson samples has steep distal retouch. The least frequent forms are those with retouch on both lateral edges. Retouch angles are steep on most specimens and tool accessory forms are relatively numerous. Fluted point forms predominate at these sites but there is a minor component of stemmed and small triangular points at Shoop. Both collections contain bifaces. Cores are abundant in the Williamson collection but do not occur at Shoop. The Williamson debitage:tool ratio is high but that for Shoop is very low.

The distribution of projectile point forms displays a moderate amount of variation between most collections. Lindenmeier, Blackwater, Shoop, and Williamson points are almost all fluted even though other forms are present in small numbers at Lindenmeier and Shoop. On the other hand, the dominant form in the Quad collection is a notched, basally thinned point often referred to as Dalton. Stemmed and lanceolate forms occur with relative frequency in this collection while fluted points are both rare and varied in form. Point forms in the Vernon collection are about equally distributed among fluted and stemmed forms. The fluted points in this collection are comparatively thick, short and not so finely made as are the so-called classic Folsom points.

Non-artifactual remains were recovered from only four sites. Extinct mammals were associated with artifacts at the Lindenmeier, Blackwater, and possibly the Horner Sites. Deer, antelope, and rabbit bones were also found at Lindenmeier. Of primary interest is the high frequency of occurrence of rabbit and rodent remains, hackberry seeds, and mussel shells at the Levi Site.

## TABLE 24
### Distribution of Tool Categories within Samples

| | low | low/stp | | steep | | 2 lat | | 1/d | 1/1 | | 1 lat | | tip | | | | |
| | I | II | V | IV | III | X | XIII | IX | VIII | VII | XI | XII | VI | N | $\bar{x}_L$ | $<\delta$ $\bar{x}_D$ |
|---|---|---|---|---|---|---|---|---|---|---|---|---|---|---|---|---|
| Lind: | 30 | 16 | 8 | 31 | 7 | 54 | — | 17 | 9 | 27 | 32 | 12 | 10 | 253 | 49° | 65° |
| Blac: | 1 | — | — | 2 | — | 5 | — | 10 | 4 | 5 | 16 | 5 | 3 | 49 | 49° | — |
| Horn: | 9 | 6 | — | 4 | — | 3 | — | 5 | 3 | 6 | 13 | 5 | 2 | 56 | 45° | 55° |
| Levi: | — | — | — | — | — | 15 | 11 | 11 | 5 | 9 | 13 | 5 | 4 | 73 | 55° | 67° |
| Shoo: | 12 | 6 | 6 | 36 | 19 | 14 | — | 6 | 3 | 34 | 2 | — | 2 | 140 | 54° | 65° |
| Will: | 4 | 10 | 4 | 12 | 2 | 2 | 4 | 2 | 2 | 14 | 10 | — | 1 | 67 | 58° | 68° |
| Quad: | 10 | 28 | 2 | 24 | 4 | 20 | 24 | 8 | 26 | 56 | 18 | 10 | 13 | 241 | 47° | 66° |
| Vern: | — | — | — | 1 | — | 4 | 2 | 2 | — | 1 | 1 | — | 1 | 12 | 51° | 60° |

low = acute distal retouch  
low/stp = acute or steep distal retouch  
steep = steep distal retouch  
2 lat = retouch on both lateral edges  
1/d = retouch on one or both lateral edges plus distal edge  
1/1 = retouch on one or both lateral edges  
1 lat = retouch on one lateral edge only  
tip = tip retouch only

## TABLE 25

### Distributions of Associated Artifacts and Non-artifactual Remains

| | POINTS | | | | | | FLAKED | | | GRIND | FAUNA | | | | | VEG |
|---|---|---|---|---|---|---|---|---|---|---|---|---|---|---|---|---|
| | | | | | | | | | | | mam | bis | | der | r/r | seeds |
| | flt | lan | stm | oth | pre | | bi | c | debi | | | ext | mod | | | |
| Lindenmeier : | 99 | 9 | — | — | + | | 30 | + | 6:1 | — | — | + | — | + | + | — |
| Blackwater : | 11 | — | — | — | — | | 7 | — | 1:1 | — | + | + | — | — | — | — |
| Horner : | — | 88 | — | — | — | | 5 | — | 3:1 | — | — | ? | ? | — | — | — |
| Levi : | — | 61 | 1 | — | ? | | 23 | + | 25:1 | + | — | ? | — | + | + | + |
| Shoop : | 39 | — | 1 | 4 | + | | 16 | — | 2:1 | — | — | — | — | — | — | — |
| Williamson : | 46 | — | — | — | + | | 18 | + | 19:1 | — | — | — | — | — | — | — |
| Quad : | 8 | 11 | 23 | 62 | + | | 31 | + | 2:1 | — | — | — | — | — | — | — |
| Vernon : | 4 | 1 | 4 | 1 | + | | 6 | + | 20:1 | + | — | — | — | — | — | — |

flt = fluted points  
lan = lanceolate points  
stm = stemmed points  
oth = other point forms  
pre = point preforms  
bi = bifaces  
c = cores  

debi = debitage:tool ratio  
mam = mammoth  
bis = bison (ext=extinct),
      (mod=modern)  
der = deer  
r/r = rabbits and rodents  
GRIND = food-grinding tools

# 6. PROCESSES OF ARTIFACT PRODUCTION

## RAW MATERIAL SELECTION

The data obtained in this study strongly suggest that those peoples whom we call Paleo-Indians employed intensive selective criteria in their search for stone materials suitable for conversion into tools. The data further suggest that Paleo-Indians could control flaking processes to such an extent that almost any kind of stone could be made to yield the desired kinds of flakes. Since this is so, the specific functional properties of flakes from certain parent materials must have been sought. It is quite clear that those stones were sought out which were most easily shaped by flaking techniques and which, when fractured, produced edge characteristics most readily useful to the tasks at hand. These latter qualities—hardness, sharpness of fractured edge, and receptiveness to modification and resharpening by flaking—were probably of primary concern in the selection of raw materials. Selection for the functional qualities inherent in the chalcedony-chert groups, those qualities just mentioned, accounts for the relative popularity of these materials at most of the sites in this survey.

This interpretation is supported by the fact that chalcedonies and cherts were often imported into sites where these materials do not occur naturally even though less desirable stones may have been available locally in quantity. The procurement of exotic materials must have entailed some effort and some sort of co-ordinating mechanism must have been developed by Paleo-Indian social groups to insure the acquisition of these materials. Direct mining expeditions, intergroup trade or some form of social exchange (e.g. marriage or gift relationships) are among those mechanisms which may have served as vehicles for exotic material distribution. It is probable that mechanisms for the procurement and distribution of raw materials were part of the social infra-structure of Paleo-Indian life. It does not appear to have been so among the majority of later peoples who were content to use, or whose requirements were well met by, a great variety of local materials.

It is interesting to note that the proportion of tools made from imported materials is generally higher at each site than is the proportion of chipping debris from these materials (Table 3). It is reasonable to assume on this basis that tools made of exotic materials were manufactured elsewhere—probably near the source of the parent material—and that they were only rejuvenated or resharpened at the site on which they were found. It is also apparent that these materials were preferred for tool use. It might be concluded that the absence in the Vernon sample of tools made from chalcedony resulted from the fact that these tools were so valuable that they were taken with the occupants when they left the site. However, such a conclusion is not justified because the site has been selectively collected by amateurs; although I have not seen these collections, I would expect to find chalcedony tools among them.

## TECHNOLOGICAL VARIATION

Formal variation in artifact morphology is the product of technological, functional, stylistic, and accidental forces which have acted upon artifacts. Accidental forces include those which lead to artifact breakage during manufacture and utilization as well as those which act upon specimens after they have been discarded. A study of artifact breakage would be interesting in itself and would no doubt contribute significantly to our understanding of artifact usage. But this will not concern us here. Stylistic variation in stone tools, as in ceramics, may be related to social partitioning within a group but such variation was not recognized in the artifacts included in this study.

Technological processes in stone tool manufacture are those which are activated in the conversion of raw stone materials into culturally useful forms. A major assumption which underlies the following discussion is that an aboriginal knapper was the cultural recipient of a specific set of stone-working processes and that he could employ these processes in the production of flakes that could be most easily and directly modified into the tools which he needed. It is apparent from the data, that any knapper in a social group occupying any site from which samples were drawn exercised controls over flaking techniques that were widely shared by other knappers in the group. Whether these controls are inherent in the processes employed or whether adjustments must be made when these processes are applied to different stone types can only be determined by experiment. Crabtree (Crabtree and Butler 1964: 1) suggests that some rocks must be heat treated before being flaked. Other technical adjustments may be necessary as well.

It seems evident, however, that flaking techniques were directed toward the production of flakes that could be converted into tools with a minimum of further modification. In almost every sample, the mean values of flake angles, medial axes, and length-width-thickness dimensions are essentially the same for tools as for that sample as a whole. Unmodified, unutilized flakes tend to vary more widely from sample means. Obviously, specific flake forms were being sought and selected for tool use. It seems reasonable to suggest that technological processes of stone flaking were directed toward the preparation of these preferred flake forms and that these forms were prescribed by functional criteria. This interpretation is supported by the fact that post-detachment modification is minimal on most tools in this series. In many cases, modification appears to have been accomplished by the simple expedient of dragging a flaking baton along one lateral edge of a flake. And in only rare cases were tools (other than points and bifaces) modified beyond the immediate area of utilization. It is significant, furthermore, that a relatively large proportion of flakes was utilized without post-detachment modification of any sort. Clearly, Paleo-Indian technological control of flaking processes was such that functionally desirable flake forms could be predetermined on and struck directly from cores.

The data suggest that striking platform architecture is of fundamental importance in predetermining at least some flake form characteristics. Overall specimen size, although probably related in part to raw material size, is also directly related to platform size. Platform thickness is apparently a strong determinant of specimen thickness and width and, to a lesser extent, of specimen length. Platform width was not tested against other variables but this dimension displays a tendency to vary within samples in a manner similar to that displayed by platform thickness. We may, therefore, conclude that platform size is a controlling factor in overall flake size. The flake angle ($\beta$) appears to be another factor upon which specimen morphology depends. Although the pattern is not consistent among all samples, the large samples and the pooled data indicate that increases in specimen thickness are strongly related to increases in the steepness of the flake angle. Specimen width is less strongly related to the flake angle and length appears to be only weakly correlated, if at all. These correlations suggest that a decision to produce thicker, heavier flakes or thinner, sharper flakes could be implemented in part by controlling the striking direction and the point of striking force application.

We may, therefore, conclude that flake morphology depends upon a number of factors. Among the most important technical factors that can be measured, platform size and striking direction appear to be critical (see correlation tables). The amount of force applied in detachment is also important, but I know of no way to measure this factor after the flake has been removed. Predetachment core surface preparation is undoubtedly a factor in determining flake form and perhaps size as well but a thorough study of this aspect of flint working would require detailed examination of the cores themselves. Unfortunately, Paleo-Indian cores are not generally available and are, therefore, excluded from this study. Non-cultural factors affecting flake size include raw material size and the degree of elasticity of the stone. While it is probably not true that a Paleo-Indian knapper could direct every single flake to a specific size and shape, it appears to be certain that he could regulate any series of flakes to meet intended dimensional and formal tolerances. He apparently did this by varying the distance from the edge of a core at which he applied detaching force as well as the direction and strength of that force.

There is some internal evidence to suggest that other characteristics of platform preparation visible on flakes are indicative of more specific core-flake relationships. Transverse preparation and platform abrasion co-occur in greatest frequency in the same samples (Table 4). These samples—Lindenmeier, Blackwater, Horner—also contain high proportions of thin flakes with small platforms and relatively acute flake angles. This combination of characteristics is indicative of a high proportion of thinning, trimming, and resharpening flakes at these sites. Transverse preparation and abrasion would be applied to relatively narrow striking areas in order to provide purchase for a detaching force to "peel" off a thin flake. The core, in this case, might be a flake undergoing modification into a tool. In many cases, abrasion may have been the product of tool use. Such an inference fits well with the previous suggestion that specimen thickness is directly related to platform thickness. A "peeling" force would necessarily be applied near the core platform edge and would, therefore, carry with it only a small flake platform remnant at the same time that it was producing a thin flake. Such a force is also likely to produce relatively high proportions of acute values of $\beta$.

Flakes with flat, relatively large platforms and comparatively steep flake angles display a lower frequency of abrasion and they are generally larger. Such flakes were probably derived from relatively large prepared cores. Flat preparation is, of course, the result of flaking and seems to have been accomplished by the removal of a large, flat flake from one end of a core; the resulting surface formed the platform from which one or more flakes were struck. The flake platform remnant is usually too small to disclose the direction of the initial preparing blow; therefore, the non-directional term *flat* is used to describe the flake platform remnant. Lateral preparation seems to be simply a form of flat preparation applied to a relatively restricted area.

Four of the flake angle and medial axis values obtained from the focal samples of this study are compared with two other samples from quite different time periods and cultural associations. Many differences and a few similarities are revealed. The two samples which are compared with the main body of data are from the Denbigh component at Cape Krusenstern, Alaska and from Big Kiokee Creek in Georgia. (Site information has been given previously.) Figure 30 summarizes the data from these samples and Table 26 lists the *t* scores of significance between all samples. Neither sample is wholly adequate but they were the best that could be obtained. In both cases, N values are low. Archaeological controls are excellent for the Denbigh sample but are non-existent for that from Big Kiokee Creek.

The data obtained from Denbigh specimens are clearly different from those obtained from all other samples. Both the flake angle and the medial axis exhibit strong tendencies to be perpendicular to the striking platform. This is suggestive of true core-blade technique. The material from which Denbigh implements are made is a flint of high quality. Unfortunately, no other characteristics of these implements were recorded. Although the evidence is scanty, it seems highly improbable that such deviant distribution profiles and mean values would be obtained if the Denbigh sample were drawn from the same technological population as were the Paleo-Indian samples. Therefore, although a number of typological similarities exist between Denbigh and the Paleo-Indian assemblages, the technological data support recent $C^{14}$ age determinations (Giddings 1964) in placing Denbigh well outside Paleo-Indian boundaries. I suggest that the typological similarities which exist among the assemblages reflect functional regularities inherent in a hunting way of life.

The Big Kiokee data are interesting in that some continuity of flaking preferences in the southeastern Woodlands are indicated. The distribution of $<\beta$ in this sample displays bimodal peaks in the same intervals in which the Quad sample reaches peaks. However, the Big Kiokee sample exhibits a greater tendency to significantly higher values of $\beta$ and the mean value of this variable for the sample reflects this tendency. The medial axis ($<\alpha$) also tends to higher values in this sample but it is not significantly different in this respect from the Quad sample. Big Kiokee artifacts are made of a variety of materials including rhyolite, quartz, and a chalky silica stone which may be a chemically altered chert. It is useful to note, furthermore, that platform preparation in the Big Kiokee sample tends to be flat (Flat = .70, Trans. = .01, Lat. = .29) and that the position of maximum flake width tends to the proximal half of specimens (0-2 = .52, 3 = .30, 4-6 = .18). There is no platform abrasion on Big Kiokee specimens. In all of these characteristics, Big Kiokee resembles Quad. The Big Kiokee Creek data suggest that flaking procedures which first became common in the early stages of human occupation in the eastern part of the United States were maintained in at least part of that region well into late prehistoric horizons.

The Vernon data may also be interpreted as indicating a technological shift toward the production of thicker, heavier tools which were needed to meet the requirements of an arid environment. Some experimentation with new materials may also be reflected in the data. It would be instructive to compare the Vernon assemblage with one from a later, full Desert Culture context. I would expect that the trends toward steeper flake angles, thicker and heavier tools, and steeper edges displayed at Vernon would be even more pronounced in the later assemblage.

## FUNCTIONAL VARIATION

Functional variation in artifacts is the product of post-detachment modification of flakes to make them more efficient in the performance of certain operations and of further alteration of the utilized edges or

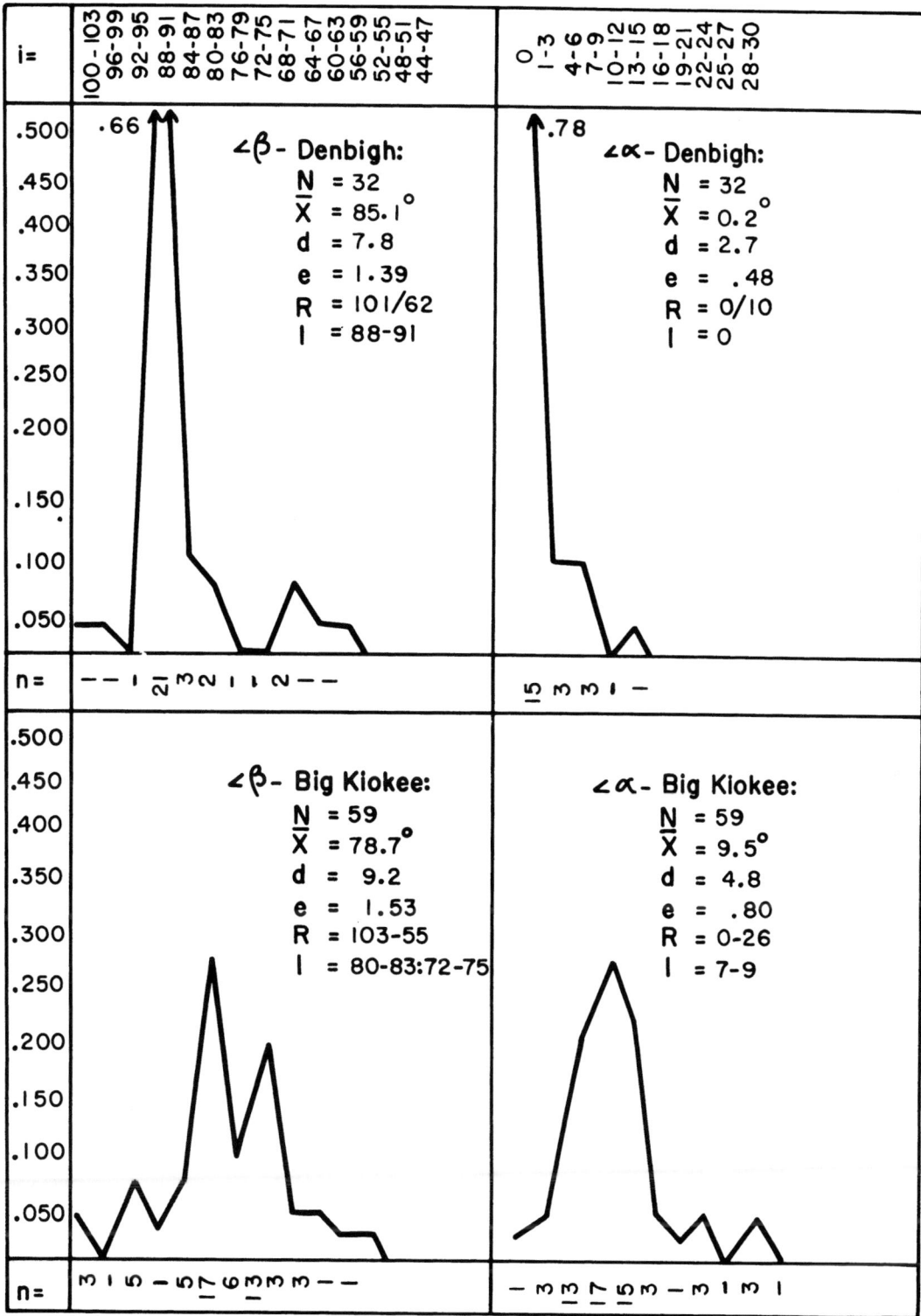

Fig. 30. Frequency distributions of $<\beta$ and $<\alpha$ for Denbigh and Big Kiokee Creek.

## TABLE 26

### Test Scores of Significance (*t*) between Site Flake Characteristics

| Variable and Site | Lindenmeier | Blackwater | Horner | Levi | Shoop | Williamson | Quad | Vernon | N | $\bar{X}$ | e |
|---|---|---|---|---|---|---|---|---|---|---|---|
| <$\beta$ (Striking Angle) | | | | | | | | | | | |
| Denbigh: | 11.29 | 12.50 | 11.65 | 10.44 | 7.83 | 8.59 | 8.33 | 8.25 | 32 | 85.1 | 1.39 |
| Big Kiokee: | 6.30 | 6.91 | 7.17 | 6.27 | 3.74 | 4.30 | 3.73 | 3.93 | 59 | 78.7 | 1.53 |
| <$\alpha$ (Medial Axis) | | | | | | | | | | | |
| Denbigh: | 7.94 | 6.21 | 6.30 | 6.95 | 6.41 | 7.64 | 6.90 | 6.87 | 32 | .2 | .48 |
| Big Kiokee: | 2.94 | 2.58 | 3.51 | 2.37 | 2.89 | 2.14 | (1.01) | 2.79 | 59 | 9.5 | .80 |

All scores significant at p = .05 except Quad x Big Kiokee (circled).

surfaces of artifacts under the stress of use. In the series of tools under consideration, modification was always accomplished by edge retouch which is, of course, a technological process and all of the considerations of the previous section apply here as well. But retouch was carried out primarily to increase the suitability of a flake for certain functional ends and it may be thought of as indicative of those ends.

The distribution of edge angle values found in the samples in this series (Figs. 17 - 24) displays a distribution with peaks in the 26° - 35°, the 46° - 55°, and the 66° - 75° range. We may reasonably suspect that differential functional capacities are reflected in this distribution. While it would certainly be an oversimplification to equate each mode with some specific functional operation, general categories of functional effectiveness may be suggested for each mode. We may infer that cutting operations are associated with the most acute mode (26° - 35°). Essentially all angles of this value occur on lateral edges. Semenov (1964: 20) suggests that the optimum angle for whittling knives is 35° - 40°. Meat and skin cutting knives may be expected to have even more acute working edges. Edge angles in this size range are often not the result of retouch but are simply the natural edges of flakes which have been utilized in an unaltered state.

The most frequent incidence of edge angle values falls within the 46° - 55° interval. The prevalence of angles of this size suggests that this was a broadly useful attribute appropriate to a number of functional applications. Angles of this size occur both on lateral and on distal edges. Inferred uses for this range of edge angle values are (1) skinning and hide scraping, (2) sinew and plant fiber shredding, (3) heavy cutting of wood, bone, or horn, and (4) tool back blunting. Large unhafted tools retouched on the distal edge and on one or both lateral edges as well as socketed endscrapers are suggested implements for the first set of tasks. The same unhafted tools and tools retouched on both lateral edges would be appropriate to the second group. Tools with natural edge angles of about 50° might have been preferred for bone cutting but edges carefully retouched to this size could also be used for this purpose. Edge blunting is common in all of the Paleo-Indian collections studied. Retouch of about 50° or more was used to create dulled edges on the backs of many cutting or scraping tools so that greater pressure could be applied to the working edges of the tools. These tools are the analogues of European Upper Paleolithic backed blades. They obviously were not hafted. Burin-like blows were also employed to blunt tool backs.

Edge angles of 66° - 75° are found on about 12 per cent of all laterally retouched tools and about 48 per cent of all distally retouched tools. Suggested functions for tools with edges in this steepness range are (1) wood working, (2) bone working, and (3) heavy shredding. It is significant that 65 per cent of all accessory tool tips and concavities are associated with tools having edge angles of this steepness. Socketed endscrapers and heavy, unhafted side tools are included in this group. A large proportion of those tools in the 56° - 65° edge angle category (present in significant quantity only in the Levi and Williamson samples) are probably functionally allied with these more steeply edged tools.

Since, as has been observed, retouch was normally held to a minimum, we may expect that the part of the artifact to which retouch was applied was carefully chosen for its mechanical qualities. Distal retouch, occurring as it does at the end of the longitudinal axis of a tool, is located at the point where the maximum mechanical advantage of the tool may be realized. Distal retouch occurs most commonly on the ends of relatively narrow and thick "blades" or "flake-blades." Tools of this sort are usually called endscrapers. Formal Categories I-V may be assigned to this class of tools. There is suggestive evidence that these tools were hafted. The stone bits of Eskimo hafted endscrapers frequently exhibit lateral edge crushing at the points where they make contact with the haft end. Paleo-Indian endscrapers often exhibit a similar condition. The haft, in the latter case, need have been no more than the severed end of a long bone into which the stone bit was socketed. The need to fit the stone tool into its socket can account for at least some of the lateral retouch found on endscrapers. Hafting, of course, increases the mechanical force which may be applied to the distal end of the bit, and since endscrapers tend to be among the smallest tools in any assemblage, their functional effectiveness probably depended upon hafting. Semenov (1964: 87) thinks that endscrapers could have been used without the aid of a haft but modifies this view (1964: 88) to suggest hafting for short specimens. I would suggest, however, that the differences in length exhibited by endscrapers—at least among North American examples—are mechanically insignificant and that we may, for the present, assume that most, if not all, tools of this type were hafted. Furthermore, the more specific term, socketed, is probably justified in describing the hafting type.

Distal retouch angles on endscrapers display a bimodal distribution of values centering on 55° and 75°. Two possible explanations for this bimodality may be advanced. Increasing steepness may be a function of resharpening as is suggested by the Lindenmeier and Quad data and it is reasonable to assume that resharpening is responsible for at least some increased steepness on individual tools. But the Shoop and Williamson samples which include high proportions of endscrapers with very steep distal retouch, do not follow this pattern. Osgood (1940: 80) notes that Ingalik endscrapers may be sharpened as many as five times during the scraping of a single caribou skin.

I would suggest that the different angle sizes are related to different functions. More acute bits, in this interpretation, would be associated with the preparation of hides and steeper bits would be associated with heavy wood and bone working. There is some evidence to support such an interpretation. Figure 31 illustrates the wear patterns associated with both forms. Notice that the Lindenmeier (Fig. 31, a) bit is polished to a high luster on the distal edge and that this luster extends onto the adjacent dorsal ridges of the distal end of the tool. The Horner artifact (Fig. 31, d) shows a similar polish on its distal end but this polish continues ventrally. Higher magnification reveals a large number of parallel striations in these polished areas (Fig. 31b, e). These striations may have been produced during the scraping of hair from skins or in working a clay or grit mixed curing agent over the skin. Semenov (1964: Fig. 31) illustrates similar striations on endscrapers from the Upper Paleolithic site of Timonovka. The fact that the polished area on some specimens extends over the dorsal rather than the ventral surface suggests that some Paleo-Indian hide scrapers were pulled over the skin with the ventral side facing the direction of motion in contrast to the recent Eskimo practice of pushing the scraper and thus producing ventral wear. As Figure 31, d clearly shows, however, some hide scrapers were also pushed in a manner similar to the Eskimo method. It is possible that both hide scraping (pulling) and softening (pushing) were accomplished with these tools. Since ventral polish has not yet been observed on Lindenmeier specimens and dorsal polish appears to be absent at Horner, we may ask if a change in

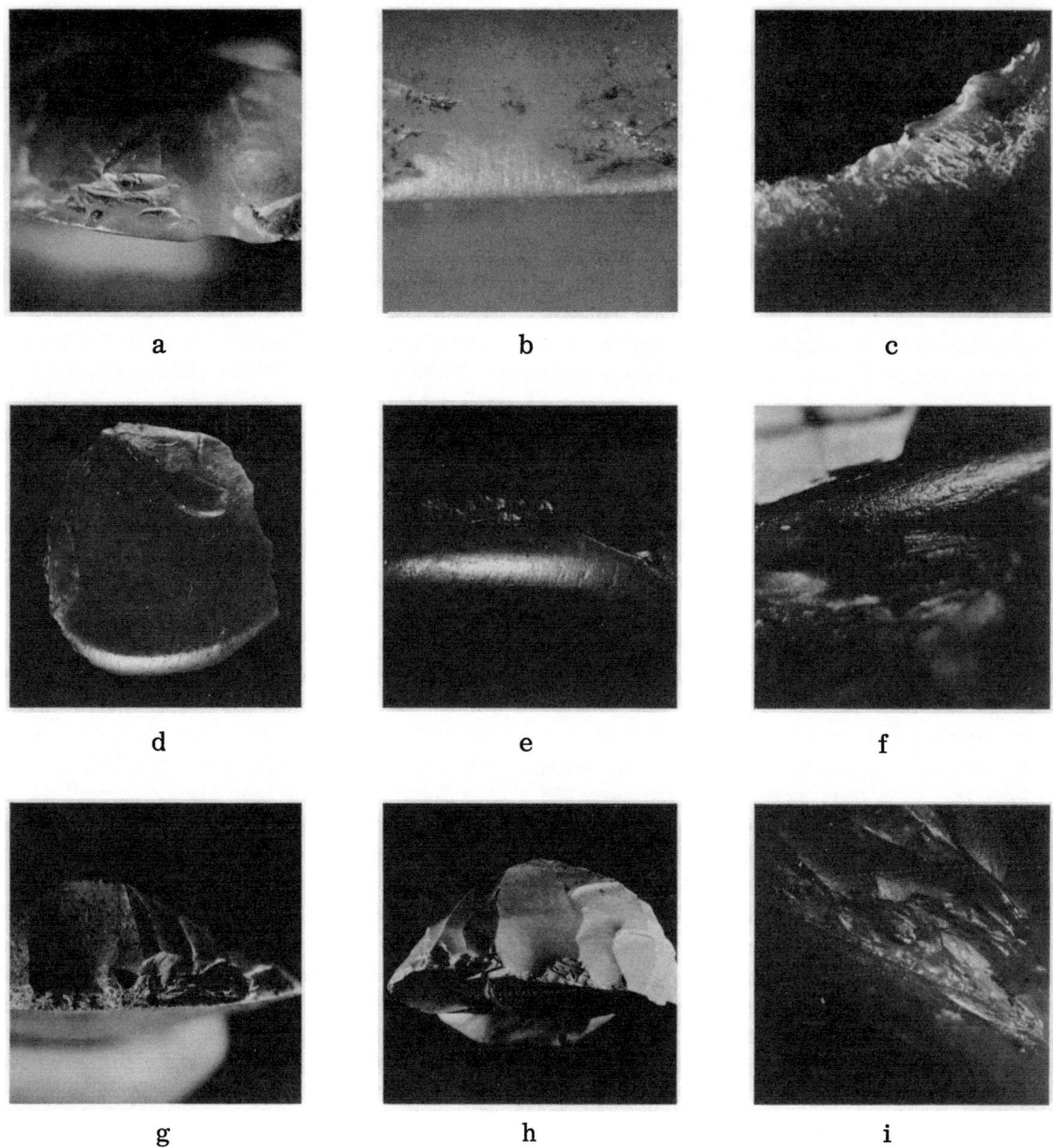

Fig. 31. Wear patterns on stone tools. $a$, endscraper distal edge, $\delta_D = 55°$, Lindenmeier; $b$, edge of $a$; $c$, lateral edge of cutting knife, $\delta_L = 25°$, Lindenmeier; $d$, ventral face of endscraper, L = 16 mm., Horner; $e$, edge of $d$; $f$, lateral edge of "sidescraper", $\delta_L = 50°$, Lindenmeier; $g$, endscraper distal end, $\delta_D = 70°$, Quad; $h$, endscraper distal end, $\delta_D = 75°$, Williamson; $i$, edge of $h$. ($b$, 25 times actual size; $c$, $e$, + $i$, five times actual size; $f$, twelve times actual size.)

endscraper use habits occurred between the one and the other. I am not prepared to answer this question on the strength of the evidence now at hand.

Steeper bits display a shattered edge that appears to consist of a stepped series of tiny chip scars which extends over the dorsal face (Fig. 31, $g$-$i$) and sometimes onto the ventral surface as well. This suggests that the tool was drawn with heavy pressure over a tough, unyielding surface somewhat in the fashion of an adze or plane. The high incidence of heavy tips and concavities associated with steep bits supports the inference that these tools were employed in the manufacture of wooden and bone implements.

It is interesting to note that Bohmers (1963) has presented evidence which suggests that northern European Upper Paleolithic and Mesolithic endscraper angles vary in the same range as do those examined in this series. He also states (1963: 469) that endscraper angles can be used to divide the Upper Paleolithic from the Epi-Paleolithic of the area although he does not expand upon this statement. His histograms, however, indicate that Upper Paleolithic angles are concentrated in the 50° - 70° range and that Mesolithic angles in the 60° - 80° range are most frequent. Unfortunately, mean values and standard deviations are not given so direct comparison with my data is not possible. Notice, however, that shifts in distal edge angle values of precisely this order of magnitude were observed between the western and the eastern sites included in this study. Figures 17 - 24 document this shift. I would suggest that in both the Mesolithic case and the North American case these shifts are the result of regularities in adaptation to increasingly wooded environments.

It should be noted, however, that a functional explanation for endscraper edge variation does not necessarily preclude a technological explanation as well. The causal factors underlying this variation may well be multiple and complex. It may be, for example, that distal angles of approximately 50° - 55° were useful for hide working, that resharpening progressively steepened these angles, and that these more steeply bitted tools were then used for different purposes such as bone and wood shaping.

A second set of distally retouched tools is large, relatively thick, and retouched on one or both lateral edges as well. Accessory tips and concavities are relatively common. Formal Category IX represents these tools. Edge angle distribution is bimodal with peaks at 45° and 65°. Resharpening may be responsible for steeper edges but it should be noted that a positive correlation between lateral angle size and artifact width and thickness is found in a number of samples (Tables 12-15). This may be taken to indicate that steeper lateral angles are to be expected naturally on heavier specimens. It is significant that this relationship appears only in samples with high proportions of heavy tools. Progressive steepening due to edge resharpening would lead to a random relationship between edge angle size and thickness when most specimens are relatively thin but, in those cases in which thick specimens are relatively numerous, a positive relationship between thickness and lateral edge size can be expected. It is suggested, therefore, that heavy flakes were produced and selected for use in those tasks which require comparative toughness rather than sharpness of edge. The tools now being considered might well have been useful in heavy butchering tasks such as carcass dismembering when they had relatively acute edges. As their edges increased in steepness (either through resharpening or through the selection of naturally steeper blanks) they may have been employed in the fleshing of hides or in heavy shredding operations. The unmodified proximal edge of such a tool with its relatively blunt platform area would provide a natural backing for the tool and permit the application of strong pressure to the working edges.

Tools with exclusively lateral retouch may be divided into two general groups—those with retouch on one edge only and those with retouch on both lateral edges. Neither group shows any indication of hafting and, although some specimens are relatively small, the large size of most of these tools would make hafting unnecessary. Tools with single edge retouch are represented by Categories VII, XI, and XII. These tools are made on large, rather thin flakes. One edge is retouched with a series of relatively broad, short flakes which produce a straight or slightly convex edge which is approximately as thick as the body of the tool itself. The size of this edge angle is about 50°. The opposite edge is unretouched but often shows wear in the form of tiny chips that have been "nibbled" or "nicked" off. Chips of this sort do not extend over either face of the tool but form a series of irregular scallops which impinge slightly on both faces (Fig. 31, c). The ridges and adjacent faces of these chips frequently show some degree of polish. The edge which displays this kind of chipping is frequently irregular in outline suggesting that it has been considerably altered by use. The utilized edge varies in size but is commonly between 30° and 50° in inclination. Accessory tips and concavities are rare in this group. I would suggest that the majority of these tools served as cutting implements and that retouching served to blunt the back edge (that edge in contact with the hand) so that increased pressure could be applied to the cutting edge without damaging the hand of the user. Tools of this kind are probably the functional equivalent of European Upper Paleolithic backed blades.

Tools with retouch on both lateral edges are generally thicker than are those with single edge retouch and they tend to be somewhat more regularly shaped. This latter factor may partly be attributed to the fact that retouching tends to regularize tool contour but a lower degree of utilization breakage may be a contributing factor as well. Tools of this kind are represented by Categories VIII, X, and XIII. Retouch on these tools is regular and, except on Category VIII specimens, always at least moderately steep. Wear, in the form of heavy, rounded abrasion of an edge, is often readily apparent on these tools. The microscopic striations which make up this abrasion frequently lie parallel to the edge (Fig. 31, $f$) rather than perpendicular to it as in the case of endscraper wear. Wear patterns of this sort are exclusively associated with small, very thick tools. These tools may have been used to cut slots or shallow grooves into wood or bone. Another type of wear associated with doubly retouched tools is a heavy, broken chipping. The heavy chipping is associated with large tools the edges of which are steeply retouched. Woodworking and heavy fiber shredding are suggested functions for these tools. Nibbling and polishing occur on broad, relatively flat tools with moderately steep edges. These tools may have been used in hide working.

Category VI represents those tools usually called gravers. The function of these tools has been the subject of controversy for some time and this study has not resolved the issue. However, a preliminary examination of the internal distribution of artifacts at the Lindenmeier site suggests that graver distribution is essentially coextensive with that of incised bone artifacts. If this distributional pattern is verified by more extensive work, it will provide strong support for the view that gravers were used to incise bone.

One other category of artifacts has received little attention in this study but it must be mentioned here. This category is that of utilized flakes. These flakes were not purposefully modified in any way after they were detached from a core but were used just as they came from a core. They all bear use marks of some sort. Most utilized edges tend to be shallow and probably occur most frequently in the $20° - 40°$ range although steeper edges occasionally display wear. Edge angles of less than $20°$ were seldom used, probably because they were too delicate to sustain any significant pressure. It is probable that most utilized flakes were used to cut meat and skins and it is possible that most cutting of this kind was done only with unaltered flakes and not with formal tools. It seems likely that any suitable flake that was readily available was utilized for a specific task and then discarded, perhaps to be used again for some later task or perhaps to be left where it fell.

# 7. SITE ACTIVITIES

Thus far, the discussion has focused primarily upon the samples of artifacts drawn from each site assemblage. A considerable amount of variation has been recognized among these samples. This inter-sample variation has been attributed to control of technological processes of artifact production and selection for functional appropriateness by the makers and users of the artifacts. If we turn now to a consideration of total assemblage configurations we may expect to gain significant insights not only into the activity patterns which formed each site but into the structure of site localization processes as well. Our attention will shift from samples to sites.

Site variation may be expected to reflect a number of interacting factors which enter into site selection and occupation. Differential cultural responses to divergent ecological opportunities should be reflected in the artifact content of sites. The size and social composition of the group which occupied a site as well as the duration and periodicity of occupation may be expected to vary among sites. The social arrangement of an aboriginal society (as of a modern society) may be expected to vary internally in relation to differential task performance requirements, the degree of mobility required to carry out an activity, and the kinds of contact maintained with other groups. Length and periodicity of occupation are in part influenced by seasonal fluctuations in resource availability and in part by long term patterns of territory occupation. The structure of this variation should be reflected in the structure of the artifact inventory. Furthermore, the kinds of activities carried out on a site will influence its structure and should be reflected in the assemblage content of the site.

Binford and Binford (1966: 268) have pointed out that there is no necessary relationship between the distribution of resources and distribution of suitable living areas in an environment. We would expect, therefore, to find that a differential distribution of sites existed in any given territory and that different activities were associated with these sites. Those sites located near available resources would be expected to yield evidence of the exploitation of those resources as the primary activity of the site. These sites may be called *Limited Activity Locations*. Those sites located in favorable camping areas would be expected to yield evidence of a variety of activities performed by a relatively larger number of people. These sites may be called *Multiple Activity Locations*. Seven of the sites considered in this study fall easily into these two groups as follows:

A. Multiple Activity Locations
   1. Lindenmeier
   2. Quad
   3. Levi
B. Limited Activity Locations
   1. Blackwater
   2. Horner
   3. Williamson
   4. Shoop

The Vernon Site is not so easily categorized.

Each of these sites will be considered separately. For each a number of questions will be asked: (1) What is the nature of the artifact composition of this site? (2) What can be said about the activities carried on at the site? (3) What can be said about the population that occupied the site? And finally, (4) are regularities apparent among the assemblages that may lead to inferences of regularities in past human behavior? The discussion which follows is strongly influenced by ideas developed in Steward (1955), Gearing (1958), and Service (1962).

## LINDENMEIER

The Lindenmeier Site has yielded a greater variety of artifacts than has any other site included in this survey. This diversity led Roberts (1936: 367) to the conclusion that Lindenmeier was occupied seasonally for relatively long periods of time. The data presented here support Roberts' conclusion and permit a more detailed account of the life of the site. The extensiveness of cultural remains suggests that many people occupied the site at once. Living area has been uncovered over 1800 x 200 feet and it is certain that parts of the site remain untouched. It is true that several components are stratigraphically segregated and that, therefore, the entire area was not occupied at one time. But most components are extensive in themselves.

The great variety of exotic materials yielded by the site, although possibly derived from sources as distant as northern Wyoming and the Texas Panhandle, need not suggest that a single group of people procured all these materials directly from the different sources. It is more reasonable to assume that different groups collected materials from known sources within their territories and that some of these materials were subsequently distributed among other associated groups. Lindenmeier may have been a common meeting place for several such groups.

In addition to exotic materials, some rocks of local origin were utilized. It is significant that only a moderate amount of debitage was recovered. Roberts' notes indicate that a certain amount of this material was discarded during excavation but even if the debitage count (6:1) is doubled (which may be a realistic correction) the higher debitage:tool ratios found in this study are not approached. Local materials account for most of the cortex flakes and for the few cores which are available. The more generalized tool types and those intended for relatively brief use were usually made of local materials while the more distinctive tools were more often made from exotic stones. There can be little question that many tools were manufactured on the site. Points in various stages of manufacture and channel flakes are abundant as are other unfinished tool forms. The fact that broken point bases are numerous suggests that projectile shafts were repaired and tips replaced. The great variety of bone tools such as eyed needles and awls permit the inference that processed skins were being converted into clothing and perhaps other articles as well.

The large numbers of points, the relatively high proportions of cutting tools and shallow-bitted endscrapers, and the quantity of associated faunal remains imply that butchering and hide working were major activities. Steeply retouched scrapers and double edged tools along with relatively high proportions of accessory tips and concavities suggest that the manufacture of tools from bone and wood was also extensively carried out. The presence of gravers as well as of incised, polished, and shaped bone implements supports this inference.

There is some suggestion of activity localization at Lindenmeier. One area, designated the Bison Pit by Roberts, yielded the remains of nine young bison and only 34 artifacts. This was definitely a kill area but there is no evidence to suggest that other activities took place here. The distribution of faunal remains is not uniform over the rest of the site. Some sections are characterized by dense concentrations of bone and others by no bone at all. Higher concentrations of debitage are associated with the bone deposits but not with those sections which are devoid of bones. Points, point fragments, and unfinished points are also associated with heavy bone concentrations as are gravers, heavy scrapers, and accessory tool forms. I would suggest that these sections were the loci of male activities associated with the manufacture and maintenance of hunting equipment made of stone and bone raw materials. Related activities such as the manufacture of decorated bone objects that may have had some social significance also took place here. The artifact concentrations in boneless sections of the site have not yielded a similar complex of tools.

In summary, the Lindenmeier site seems to have been a multiband campsite which was occupied seasonally for extensive periods (perhaps as much as a month or more) at a time. Several generations may have elapsed between the earliest and latest occupations. The resident bands may have gathered in order to cooperate in bison or antelope hunts (it must be remembered that antelope and deer as well as bison are well represented in the faunal assemblage). While together, the members of the bands may have exchanged raw materials, perhaps tool blanks, and possibly mates as well. Small game and deer were also hunted. It may be that the procurement of hides was a major motivation for selection of the site since it is located near the habitats of both deer and antelope. The skins of these animals are more suitable for clothing than is the heavier bison skin. There is extensive evidence of skin working at the site. Stone quarrying was also carried out and plant materials were probably harvested. Roberts (1936: 37) has suggested a late summer or fall occupation. This appears to be a reasonable suggestion.

## QUAD

The Quad Site is the only other site in this series that has yielded as varied a stone artifact inventory as has Lindenmeier. Bone, either worked or unworked, is missing, however, probably because of soil conditions unfavorable to its preservation. The artifacts were found in small, highly concentrated clusters most of which were widely separated from each other. This concentration in relatively small areas suggests that Quad was periodically occupied by small groups rather than by a large group at one time. The very low debitage:tool ratio (2:1) may be accounted for by assuming that very little stone working was carried on at the site. The scarcity of unfinished implements at the site tends to support this assumption. Sampling error may contribute to this low ratio but a very large increase in waste flake numbers would be required to significantly alter the ratio. We may reasonably conclude that tools were brought to the site in an essentially completed state and that little stone working other than tool reconditioning was done on the site.

Quad artifact category and edge angle variation tends to conform rather closely to that found at Lindenmeier. We may, then, draw the same conclusions concerning the activities performed at Quad as we did for those at Lindenmeier. There are, however, three tool characteristics which are common in the Quad assemblage but extremely rare at Lindenmeier. The first of these is bifacial edge retouch and the second is a tendency for tool width to reach a maximum near the proximal end of the specimen. The third is a tendency of flakes and tools to display high medial axis values. This suggests that a higher frequency of "side-blow" flakes was being produced. These characteristics are common in later inventories associated with Archaic and Woodland Cultures and tend to support the view that the Quad assemblage was deposited over a long period of time. It should be remembered that the Big Kiokee Creek assemblage, probably of Woodland origin, displays these same characteristics. Soday (1954: 16) has suggested that the high degree of typological diversity displayed by the points found at Quad also suggests a very long period of occupation.

The Quad Site, then, appears to have been occupied by no more than a single band at a time. Occupation occurred periodically, perhaps over a period of several thousand years. The earliest inhabitants made fluted and basally thinned projectile points and probably followed a hunting way of life rather like that described for Lindenmeier. The first occupation does not constitute the major component of the site. Later inhabitants also hunted intensively as is seen in the large numbers of projectile points which they left behind. But there was also dependence upon plant product collecting. The generally steep distal retouch and the high proportion of heavy doubly retouched tools suggests wood working or fiber shredding. Whether this kind of activity became more important with succeeding occupations cannot be determined from the data at hand. But a selection for heavier, thicker tools made from flakes with steeper flake angles and greater lateral inclination is a major characteristic of the site. We may assume that this selection was in response to the increased desirability of such characteristics brought about by an increasing exploitation of a forest-riverine ecology (cf. Caldwell 1958).

# LEVI

The Levi Site is different from all other sites included in this study in that it is located in a natural rock shelter. Several cultural zones are stratigraphically superimposed; the sample for this study was drawn from the richest of these—Zone IV. The shelter itself and the occupied area within it are small. The occupied area could not have greatly exceeded 50 or 60 square meters and, therefore, the number of people in residence at any one time could not have been great. Naroll (1962) has suggested an average living space requirement of approximately 10 square meters per resident and on this basis we may suppose that no more than four to seven people occupied the site at one time. One hearth was found near the center of the zone under consideration; no other hearths were found. The cultural materials of Zone IV were probably deposited during a single occupation or at most during a small number of occupations over only a very few years. This interpretation is at variance with the great spread of radiocarbon dates from the zone. But these dates are stratigraphically incompatible among themselves and are derived from mussel and snail shells (Alexander 1963: 513), materials which are subject to substantial fluctuation in radiological stability. In any case, although the mussel shells were no doubt culturally introduced, the cultural significance of the snail shells which form a major part of the dating material has not been established. The presence of these shells may be more properly attributed to the moist conditions associated with travertine deposition on the shelter wall than to cultural importation. I suggest that the shelter, although obviously occupied a number of times at fairly widespread intervals, was probably occupied but once during the time represented by Zone IV deposition and that, therefore, the sample upon which this study is based was drawn from a single cultural event.

Endscrapers (Formal Tool Categories I - V) of any sort are conspicuously absent from the Levi Site. The assemblage is characterized by a very low proportion of thin-edged, sharp, cutting tools and by high proportions of steep, double- and single-edged tools. Very steep edge retouch is common. This suggests that hunting and butchering were not important activities at the site. Skin dressing would have been impractical in any case because of the small amount of space available. Deer and other ruminants may have been hunted but butchered elsewhere and only the desired parts brought to the camp.

The artifact assemblage suggests that plant products were processed on the site. The heavy tools are well suited to the task of cutting and shaping plant fibers and wood into implements. Alexander (1963: 522) suggests that the many fire-hardened, tubular, clay fragments found in the site may have been used in the fire tempering of implements made of wood or cane. The numerous burins and burin spalls may also have been utilized in wood working.

Flint working was also extensively carried on and the nearby deposits of high quality flint were probably a major attraction in the selection of the site for occupation. The very high debitage:tool ratio (25:1) and the presence of many cores indicate that all steps in flint working were performed. The high frequency of cortex and trimming flakes supports this inference. Many of the bifaces which have been called knives may, in fact, be point preforms. The presence of finished as well as unfinished points suggests that these tools were being manufactured, possibly for use elsewhere. It is probable that other tools were also made primarily for future use and taken from the site. It seems clear that the flint nodules which are common in nearby creek beds were of primary importance to the resident population.

We may conclude that the Levi Site was a short term camping place for a band segment consisting of no more than a single nuclear family or a small work party of four to seven individuals. Occupation may have recurred seasonally but, in the zone in which we are interested, the site was returned to for only a few years, if at all. The primary activities carried on were centered about raw material gathering and processing. Local flint deposits and plant resources were major attractions. Shell fish were an important food resource and may well have been gathered at the same time that raw flint nodules were being collected. Hunting was directed primarily toward small mammals such as rabbits and rodents. Hackberry seeds are present in quantity in the site and may have been important in the diet of its inhabitants. Seed-grinding stones are present. According to the records of the Department of Botany, U.S. National Museum, hackberry seeds (*Celtis reticulata Torr.*) ripen in central Texas from late September until early November. It is suggested that the Levi Site was occupied at this time of the year.

## BLACKWATER

All of the available evidence suggests that the Clovis component at Blackwater Draw represents a kill and butchering site. Warnica (1966: 348) has suggested that the differential preservation of individual mammoths indicates that a number of different kill episodes are recorded and this would seem to be a reasonable inference. The majority of the tools are retouched on one edge only or on both lateral and distal edges. These tools suggest that cutting and skinning operations constituted the major activity of the site. The majority of edge angle values fall into the inferred cutting tool category. Haury, Sayles, and Wasley (1959: 27-30) have presented a discussion of kill activities at the Lehner Site. It is possible that the events recorded at Blackwater Draw took place in a similar fashion. The almost complete absence of skin processing tools (Table 24) may be explained by the fact that elephant hide is almost useless for cultural purposes.

Warnica has also suggested that camp debris is included in the Blackwater Clovis assemblage but this does not appear to be the case. All of the debitage recovered appears to have resulted from the resharpening which was necessary to rejuvenate tools dulled during butchering operations. The extremely low debitage:tool ratio (1:1) is strong counterevidence to any suggestion that tools were manufactured on the site. No unfinished tools have been recovered. Other tools, which have been called hammerstones, cores, and broken pebbles, may well have been employed in heavy butchering tasks to break limb or rib joints and to prepare bones for marrow extraction. Frison (1967) has presented an excellent analysis of such activities at a bison kill site in Wyoming. The few gravers and two small sandstone grinding tools found at Blackwater suggest that some bone working, perhaps only of a resharpening character, may have been performed on the site.

Camps sites were undoubtedly located within the immediate vicinity of the kills but these camps were probably only work camps and they were probably occupied for no longer than the few days needed to process the butchered meat for transport. Clovis hunters probably did not engage extensively in any other activity while the kill was being processed. Work camps of this kind leave little impression on the ground. The evidence does not permit an extensive statement about the social group represented at Blackwater. It is safe to assume that several men were involved in the killing of a mammoth. But whether these men were members of a single band or of several associated bands and whether they were acting alone as a hunting party or in conjunction with other members of the larger social group remains unclear.

## HORNER

The Horner Site also was a kill and butchering site. Lateral edge angle values and laterally retouched tool types are strongly indicative of cutting and skinning operations. But, in contrast to Blackwater, hide working was also an important activity at Horner as is indicated by the high proportion of Category I and II endscrapers in the assemblage. These tools frequently display a very strong polish on their distal edges. Jepsen (1953) has suggested a late fall or early winter kill. Bison pelts are at their prime in this season and it is likely that Horner represents an annual harvest of fresh pelts for conversion into warm winter robes. No other activities seem to have been carried on to any appreciable extent. It is possible that two different kill episodes are represented; bones are concentrated in two distinct areas. But it is also possible that this distribution is an artifact of a single kill and butchering event. In either case, the number of animals slain was large (total of 180). This fact allows us to infer that more than one single band of hunters was involved and the inferred emphasis on hide working suggests that women as well as men were present. The Horner Site, then, may depict a seasonal, multiband bison hunt and hide harvest in which the entire social unit cooperated. I would suggest that site occupation was short and perhaps not repeated in the same location.

## SHOOP

Artifacts at the Shoop Site occur in eleven isolated concentrations. These concentrations are widely separated from each other and each is about 70 square meters in size. We may, therefore, conclude that the site was occupied on at least eleven different occasions and that the relatively small extent of each occupation area indicates an occupying unit of band segment size. Occupation was probably seasonal and of short duration. The same band segment may have returned periodically to the site.

The Shoop assemblage suggests a limited variety of activities. There was little stone working. Although some point blanks may have been converted to finished points, stone working appears to have been largely confined to resharpening already completed tools. This assessment is in agreement with Witthoft (1952: 479). Some hunting and skin working is indicated by a small but significant number of endscrapers and cutting tools with relatively sharp edges. The very rough nature of the terrain which is repeatedly noted by Witthoft leads to the inference that deer rather than flatland grazers were being hunted. The inferred smallness of the occupying group is in keeping with this kind of hunting.

The great majority of Shoop tools have steeply retouched edges (Figs. 17 - 24). My measurements and Witthoft's (1952: 478) observations are in agreement on this point. Tools of this sort are indicative of plant-processing operations and at Shoop emphasis may have been on the manufacture of wooden implements. The relatively high incidence of heavy tool accessory tips and concavities support this inference (Table 8).

## WILLIAMSON

This site is primarily a quarry site as was recognized by its discoverer (McCary 1951). Many chert cores have been found. Some of these are huge; the largest weighs about 45 pounds. Many large flakes struck from these cores were also present as were thousands of smaller flakes (debitage:tool ratio is 19:1). The chert material occurs in nodules of varying size and is probably derived from limestone outcrops in the nearby streambed. Quarry debris was scattered over a long distance along a ridge overlooking the stream and this suggests that the site was visited repeatedly over a fairly long period of time. Nothing can be said about the nature of the social groups which occupied the site because details of artifact distribution are lacking.

Secondary activities at the Williamson Site were centered about stone tool manufacturing and plant material processing. The large number of unfinished fluted points suggests that points were being made. The high proportion of steep-edged tools and tool accessory forms leads me to the conclusion that wooden artifacts were also being made. I would suggest that stone points were being manufactured and fitted onto shafts at the site. Other tools, especially endscrapers, were also being made. Those which were found on the site were probably worn beyond further use and the great majority of still useful tools was undoubtedly taken from the site for use elsewhere. Hunting probably was carried on only to the extent necessary to maintain the group in residence. The few broken but finished points and the small, sharp-edged cutting tool component were probably used in killing and butchering animals for immediate consumption.

## VERNON

The full range of cultural activities represented at the Vernon Site cannot be reconstructed with confidence. The tool inventory is small and incomplete. Tools in amateur collections would, if available, probably add to our understanding of the site. It is clear from the amount of debitage present, that stone working was important. The presence of basal fragments of projectile points indicates that hunting was routine and that projectiles were repaired, if not initially manufactured, at the site. The distribution of edge angles permits the inference that both butchering and plant material processing was carried on but the extent of these activities is not clear. The presence of food-grinding stones suggests that seeds were processed and consumed.

The site is extensive but thinly populated by artifacts. Human population was probably correspondingly thin. Longacre (1963) has suggested a double occupation the two elements of which are arealy distinct. His assessment seems to be correct. But the relationship between the two groups appears to be more complex than he has suggested. Technologically the materials from the southern occupational area upon which this study is based are different from the fluted point assemblages of the High Plains. But the presence of unfinished, fluted point preforms in this sample introduces the possibility that fluting techniques were known to the people who occupied this area. It is possible that no great period of time separated the two occupations and that the site records two episodes as hunters who used fluted points adapted themselves to a more intensive small game and plant orientation. The reasons behind this reorientation are not revealed by the evidence at hand.

The relative abundance of basalt specimens in the Vernon sample suggests that selective criteria were relaxed at this site, possibly in the face of difficulties encountered in the procurement of more suitable raw materials. The fact that the mean flake angle found on Vernon tools is essentially the same as that found on Lindenmeier tools, coupled with the additional fact that this angle does not vary significantly between basalt and chert specimens within the Vernon sample itself, together suggest that the same flake properties were being sought from both types of materials. It should be noted that within the two excavated areas (both in the southern half of the site), the distribution of basalt specimens is coextensive with that of chert specimens—81 per cent of the former and 84 per cent of the latter co-occur in 11 of the 80 excavated squares. It is obvious that both types of materials were in simultaneous use. But the distribution of values of the flake angle on basalt specimens is more diffuse than it is on chert specimens (both the high and the low values were obtained from basalt specimens and the modal peak is flatter for basalt). Basalt specimens are also responsible for the general overall smallness of Vernon specimens. Furthermore, basalt edges become dull rapidly and are not easily resharpened. We may conclude, therefore, that the Vernon Site was occupied by a people who preferred chert for their tools but who could, if necessary make use of basalt. They were sufficiently familiar with basalt to use it but they could not control the flaking process as completely as they could on other materials. And they no doubt found the cutting and scraping edges of their basalt tools to be less reliable than those of their chert tools.

# 8. STRUCTURE IN PALEO-INDIAN CULTURE

Although Paleo-Indian sites are usually thought of as locations where large animals were killed and butchered, only two of the eight sites examined in this study may be characterized as such. Most workers in the field of Paleo-Indian Culture are preoccupied with gross projectile point typology, chronology, and extinct megafauna; and, while their efforts have securely established the temporal position and faunal associations of the Paleo-Indian Stage, it has been difficult, from such a theoretical orientation, to formulate inferences other than those stressing the simple fact of hunting. Now that the relative status of the Paleo-Indian Stage has been fixed we have an opportunity to inquire more deeply into the nature of Paleo-Indian life. And, indeed, it is because of its early date that this stage takes on a special significance for Americanist studies. For Paleo-Indians were the first widely successful, if not the initial, human inhabitants of the North American continent and we may assume that a significant, but as yet undefined, portion of later American cultural development stemmed from this early culture.

It should come as no surprise that Paleo-Indian life, as any cultural life, was more complex than is implied by preoccupation with but one of its multivariate facets. Haury (1962), among others, has recognized the fact that hunting and plant gathering are not necessarily mutually exclusive economic pursuits. Hunting was, no doubt, a basic activity, but the fact that other activities are represented at least equally strongly in our sample of sites suggests that the organization of Paleo-Indian life included a diversified set of structural poses through which responses to ecological conditions were initiated. A number of processes were undoubtedly involved in the formation of these poses. Among them are those which structure the localization of social groups, those which structure group social organization, and those which structure subsistence and task performance activities.

## LOCALIZATION OF PALEO-INDIAN GROUPS

Processes of localization relate group activity to factors of resource availability and living-space requirements. As indicated earlier, desirable resources and suitable living areas do not always co-occur. Consequently, the structural poses assumed by a hunting-gathering society will vary according to group choices made in relating cultural activities to specific ecological conditions.

The data suggest that one mechanism for resolving this choice involved the segmentation of bands into smaller structural elements. Paleo-Indian groups apparently could accommodate the size of their operative units to meet a variety of ecological-functional conditions. It is clear that Paleo-Indian group localization was structured, in part at least, by variations in resource availability and that food animal resources were only one of these. Lee (1967) estimates that the presence of animals ranks third among Kalahari Bushman localization criteria; social considerations and the availability of vegetable food are more important. Bushman ethnography is not necessarily a valid model for Paleo-Indian reconstructions but it does suggest that these modern hunter-gatherers apply multiple criteria in the selection of sites. We may assume that earlier people also did so. Certainly the presence of large quantities of desirable stone raw materials at Williamson and Levi was a strong motivating factor in the settlement of these sites. Artifact indications are that hunting was only secondarily engaged in at these sites. The Lindenmeier, Blackwater, and Shoop data suggest that favored materials were carried for great distances and probably used a number of times along the way. Activities at Williamson, Levi, and Shoop were apparently strongly plant product oriented. Only at Blackwater and Horner were activities associated with megafauna hunting exclusively carried out and, although hunting of a number of different animal species was a major activity at Lindenmeier, quarrying, stone working, and plant processing were also important.

Paleo-Indian site interrelations appear to have been built around a series of successively larger structural units. Band segments consisting of nuclear or small extended families occupied small sites briefly and repeatedly on a seasonal basis. A limited set of activities characterize these sites. Periodically, band segments came together into full band units to engage in a greater variety of functional and social actions. Finally, several bands would sometimes meet in ecologically favorable places and cooperatively carry out a wide range of exploitative and social activities.

## SOCIAL INTEGRATION

The nature of Paleo-Indian social integration was not strongly revealed by my handling of the data. This is partly so because the data were themselves inadequate. In most cases, precise provenience data were neither observed nor recorded in the field. There are in a number of cases, however, clues to the gross size of occupying units which may be combined with suggested site activity patterns to yield speculative suggestions concerning the nature of occupying social units. I have already suggested that Lindenmeier was occupied simultaneously by a number of associated and possibly related bands. This multiband unit was made up of several nuclear families. Unlike the modern Northern Déné "macrocosmic bands," whose members are said to have only a vague sense of mutual affiliation (Helm 1961: 167), Paleo-Indian multiband units were probably closely affiliated functional units.

The basic structural unit of Paleo-Indian life, as among modern Déné, was probably the band, "a group of people who travelled and camped together, sharing the take of large game in common" (J. H. MacNeish 1956: 134). The Quad and Vernon Sites may have been occupied by groups of this kind. In addition, hunting or work parties of men and gathering parties of women may have been formed when a band or multiband unit was assembled. In short, we may accept the general statements made by Steward (1938) and Service (1962) about hunter-gatherer band organization, but the details of Paleo-Indian social life remain obscure. Steward (1938: 230-7) has documented the variability of Basin Shoshoni band unit association. Patterns of association were altered by fluctuations in resource availability, by the proximity of cooperating groups, and by the distribution of experienced hunting leaders among different groups. Paleo-Indian band association may have been affected by a similar set of factors.

## SUBSISTENCE AND TASK PERFORMANCE

Subsistence and task performance processes are intimately related to the structure of group localization. Primary among these processes are those which are directly related to the choice of a particular site. A second set of processes is centered around tool manufacture and maintenance required to perform the primary tasks as well as other activities ancillary to those tasks. A third group of processes includes those employed in sustaining the group regardless of its specific location. These include food preparation and consumption, procurement of water, manufacture and repair of clothing, and a host of everyday tasks.

Paleo-Indian bands probably behaved not unlike later hunter-gatherer groups in adjusting their behavior to their environments. Band movements were likely within a more or less well defined territory. Even during the initial spread of peoples over the continent, groups probably moved in relation to other groups and new territory was entered only as it became familiar and as population size could accommodate new ground. Bands appear to have broken up periodically either under the stress of seasonal fluctuations in resources or to more efficiently take advantage of ecological opportunities. Surface quarrying and plant collecting do not require large numbers of workers to be carried out effectively. It may be that one segment of a band exploited one set of resources while other segments directed their attention to different parts of the environment. Band segments regathered periodically and, in fact, bands themselves appear to have joined with other bands (as at Lindenmeier) in order to exploit the larger environment and to maintain socioeconomic integration. Hunting parties as well as raw material and plant collection parties may have voluntarily moved out from these larger units and returned to distribute the products of their activities to the group as a whole. It may be that mammoth and bison hunts were carried out principally by groups such as these at times when large band units were assembled.

Multiband units also functioned to maintain technocultural processes among groups and to disseminate change which arose in these processes. When individual groups moved into new environments they began to exploit the new opportunities offered by these environments and adapted their technologies to new exploitative tasks. It is probable that these adaptations involved no more than a realignment of emphasis in a pre-existing technocultural system. Those elements in a familiar technology which were most useful in the new environment were emphasized. Prolonged emphasis in one direction gradually produced a technology which was distinctive from the parent, other directed, technology. The dynamics of this process may be seen in the eastern sites included in this survey. Technologically, Shoop, Williamson, and Quad tend to be alike. To a lesser extent, they share technological features with Levi but they deviate sharply from Lindenmeier, Blackwater, and Horner. Functionally, Shoop, Williamson, Quad, and Levi are alike. These sites exemplify the tendency of a basic stone-working tradition to be modified to meet new conditions. The implication is that woodland or scrub forest conditions were being increasingly met. This need not imply any real climatic change. It is more likely that these environmental areas were entered for the first time. Structurally related changes in other sectors of the cultural system no doubt took place along with these technological changes but these changes are not discernible in the existing data. MacNeish (1964) and Flannery (1966) have suggested that postglacial adaptations were complex and not necessarily centered about the extinction of megafauna. It is probable that hunting activities at Shoop and Williamson as at Levi were directed toward small mammals and deer. These hunting patterns, once established, were maintained well into historic times. The Big Kiokee data suggest that once a basic technological adjustment to the eastern Woodlands environment had been made, it remained stable for a long period of time. A similar case may be proposed for Vernon.

Stability in basic patterns of technological and functional variation is also exemplified in the Blackwater and Horner Sites. Blackwater is the oldest and Horner among the youngest sites in our sample; some 4,000 years separate them in time. At both, large mammals were killed and butchered and this functional regularity is reflected in artifact assemblages of both. Stylistic variation is present in projectile points and as yet unrecognized structural changes may differentiate the two sites. But those technological and functional processes associated with hunting appear to have remained essentially stable.

In summary, it is clear that technological, functional, social, and ecological processes were structurally interrelated in the Paleo-Indian cultural system. Technological procedures were directed toward an economy of tool production in which functionally useful artifacts were produced with a minimum of effort. Changes in resource patterns elicited changes in functional responses and patterns of sociocultural interaction were adapted to ecological opportunities and task performance requirements. The full nature of Paleo-Indian life has yet to be worked out, but the picture of a varied subsistence economy, a simply structured social organization, and a sophisticated technocultural system begins to emerge.

# REFERENCES

ALEXANDER, HERBERT L., JR.
    1963  The Levi Site: A Paleo-Indian Campsite in Central Texas. *American Antiquity*, Vol. 28, No. 4, pp. 510-28. Salt Lake City.

ASCHER, ROBERT and MARCIA ASCHER
    1965  Recognizing the Emergence of Man. *Science*, Vol. 147, No. 3655, pp. 243-50. Washington.

BARNES, ALFRED S.
    1939  The Differences between Natural and Human Flaking on Prehistoric Flint Implements. *American Anthropologist*, Vol. 41, No. 1, pp. 99-112. Menasha.

BINFORD, LEWIS R.
    1962  Archaeology as Anthropology. *American Antiquity*, Vol. 28, No. 2, pp. 217-25. Salt Lake City.
    1964  A Consideration of Archaeological Research Design. *American Antiquity*, Vol. 29, No. 4, pp. 425-41. Salt Lake City.
    1965  Archaeological Systematics and the Study of Cultural Process. *American Antiquity*, Vol. 31, No. 2, pp. 203-10. Salt Lake City.

BINFORD, LEWIS R. and SALLY R. BINFORD
    1966  A Preliminary Analysis of Functional Variability in the Mousterian of Levallois Facies. In "Recent Studies in Paleoanthropology," edited by J. Desmond Clark and F. Clark Howell, pp. 238-95. *Special Publication of the American Anthropological Association*, Vol. 68, No. 2, Pt. 2. Menasha.

BOHMERS, A.
    1963  A Statistical Analysis of Flint Artifacts. In *Science in Archaeology*, edited by Don Brothwell and Eric Higgs, pp. 469-81. New York.

BREW, J. OTIS
    1946  Archaeology of Alkali Ridge, Southeastern Utah. *Papers of the Peabody Museum of American Archaeology and Ethnology*, Vol. 21. Cambridge.

BRYAN, KIRK and LOUIS L. RAY
    1940  Geologic Antiquity of the Lindenmeier Site in Colorado. *Smithsonian Miscellaneous Collections*, Vol. 99, No. 2. Washington.

CALDWELL, JOSEPH R.
    1958  Trend and Tradition in the Prehistory of the Eastern United States. *Memoirs of the American Anthropological Association*, No. 88. Menasha.

CAMBRON, JAMES W. and DAVID C. HULSE
    1960  An Excavation on the Quad Site. *Tennessee Archaeologist*, Vol. 16, No. 1, pp. 14-26. Knoxville.

CHANDLER, R. H.
    1929  On the Clactonian Industry at Swanscombe. *Proceedings of the Prehistoric Society of East Anglia*, Vol. 6, Part 2, pp. 79-93. Ipswich.

CHILDE, VERE GORDON
    1923  *The Dawn of European Civilization.* Kegan Paul, London.
    1936  *Man Makes Himself.* The Rationalist Press Association, London.

CLARK, J. DESMOND and F. CLARK HOWELL, editors
    1966  Recent Studies in Paleoanthropology. *Special Publication of the American Anthropological Association*, Vol. 68, No. 2, Pt. 2. Menasha.

COFFIN, ROY G.
    1937  Northern Colorado's First Settlers. [*Colorado State College,* Ft. Collins].
    1951  Sources and Origin of Northern Colorado Artifact Materials. *Southwestern Lore*, Vol. 17, No. 1. Boulder.

COTTER, JOHN
    1938  The Occurrence of Flints and Extinct Animals in Pluvial Deposits near Clovis, New Mexico. *Proceedings of the Philadelphia Academy of Natural Sciences,* Vol. 90, pp. 113-7. Philadelphia.

CRABTREE, DON E. and B. ROBERT BUTLER
    1964  Notes on Experiments in Flint Knapping: 1, Heat Treatment of Silica Minerals. *Tebiwa,* Vol. 7, No. 1, pp. 1-3. Pocatello.

DEETZ, JAMES
    1965  The Dynamics of Stylistic Change in Arikara Ceramics. *Illinois Studies in Anthropology,* No. 4. Urbana.

FLANNERY, KENT V.
    1966  The Postglacial "Readaptation" as Viewed from Mesoamerica. *American Antiquity,* Vol. 31, No. 6, pp. 800-5. Salt Lake City.

FREEMAN, LESLIE G., JR. and JAMES A. BROWN
    1964  Statistical Analysis of Carter Ranch Pottery. In "Chapters in the Prehistory of Eastern Arizona, II," by Paul S. Martin and others, pp. 125-54. *Fieldiana: Anthropology,* Vol. 55. Chicago.

FRISON, GEORGE C.
    1968  A Functional Analysis of Certain Chipped Stone Tools. *American Antiquity*, Vol. 33, No. 2, pp. 149-55, Salt Lake City.

GEARING, FRED
    1958  The Structural Poses of 18th Century Cherokee Villages. *American Anthropologist,* Vol. 60, No. 6, pp. 1148-57. Menasha.

    1962  Priests and Warriors. *Memoirs of the American Anthropological Association,* No. 93. Menasha.

GIDDINGS, J. LOUIS
    1951  The Denbigh Flint Complex. *American Antiquity,* Vol. 16, No. 3, pp. 193-203. Salt Lake City.

    1964  *The Archeology of Cape Denbigh.* Brown University Press, Providence.

HAURY, EMIL W.
    1962  The Greater American Southwest. In "Courses Toward Urban Life," edited by Robert J. Braidwood and Gordon R. Willey, pp. 106-31. *Viking Fund Publications in Anthropology,* No. 32. New York.

HAURY, E. W., E. B. SAYLES, and W. W. WASLEY
    1959  The Lehner Mammoth Site. *American Antiquity,* Vol. 25, No. 1, pp. 2-30. Salt Lake City.

HAYNES, C. VANCE
    1964  Fluted Projectile Points: Their Age and Dispersion. *Science,* Vol. 145, No. 3639, pp. 1408-13. Washington.

HAYNES, C. V. and G. A. AGOGINO
    1960  Geological Significance of a New Radiocarbon Date from the Lindenmeier Site. *Proceedings of the Denver Museum of Natural History,* No. 9. Denver.

HELM, JUNE
    1961  The Lynx Point People: The Dynamics of a Northern Athapaskan Band. *National Museum of Canada Bulletin,* No. 176. Ottawa.

HESTER, JAMES J.
    MS  Blackwater Locality No. 1: A Stratified Early Site in Eastern New Mexico. Manuscript at the University of Colorado, Boulder.

HOWARD, EDGAR BILLINGS
    1935  Evidence of Early Man in North America. *The Museum Journal,* Vol. 24, Nos. 2-3, pp. 61-171. Philadelphia.

JEPSEN, GLENN L.
    1951  Ancient Buffalo Hunters in Wyoming. *Archaeological Society of New Jersey Newsletter,* No. 24. pp. 22-4. Trenton.

    1953  Ancient Buffalo Hunters of Northwestern Wyoming. *Southwestern Lore,* Vol. 19, No. 2, pp. 19-25. Boulder.

KROEBER, A. L. and C. M. KLUCKHOHN
    1952  *Culture: A Critical Review of Concepts and Definitions.* Vintage Books, New York.

LEE, RICHARD B.
    1967 !Kung Bushman Subsistance Ecology and Group Structure. Columbia University Seminar in Ecological Systems and Cultural Evolution.

LONGACRE, WILLIAM A.
    1963 CNHM Surface Investigations of a Preceramic Site (LS-187), East Central Arizona. Paper read at 28th Annual Meeting of the Society for American Archaeology. Boulder.

MACNEISH, JUNE HELM
    1956 Leadership among the Northern Athabaskans. *Anthropologica,* No. 2, pp. 131-58. Ottawa.

MACNEISH, RICHARD S.
    1964 Ancient Mesoamerican Civilization. *Science*, Vol. 143, No. 3606, pp. 531-7. Washington.

MARTIN, PAUL SIDNEY, JOHN B. RINALDO, WILLIAM A. LONGACRE, LESLIE G. FREEMAN, JR., JAMES A. BROWN, RICHARD H. HEVLEY, and M. E. COOLEY.
    1964 Chapters in the Prehistory of Eastern Arizona, II. *Fieldiana: Anthropology,* Vol. 55. Chicago.

MCCARY, BEN C.
    1951 A Workshop Site of Early Man in Dinwiddie County, Virginia. *American Antiquity,* Vol. 17, No. 1, pp. 9-17. Salt Lake City.

NAROLL, RAOUL
    1962 Floor Area and Settlement Population. *American Antiquity,* Vol. 27, No. 4, pp. 587-9. Salt Lake City.

OSGOOD, CORNELIUS
    1940 Ingalik Material Culture. *Yale University Publications in Anthropology,* No. 22. New Haven.
    1951 Culture: Its Empirical and Nonempirical Character. *Southwestern Journal of Anthropology.* Vol. 7, No. 2, pp. 202-14. Albuquerque.

PATERSON, T. T.
    1937 Studies on the Palaeolithic Succession in England. *Proceedings of the Prehistoric Society,* Vol. 3, Part 1, pp. 87-135. Cambridge.

RADCLIFFE-BROWN, A. R.
    1933 *The Andaman Islanders.* University Press, Cambridge.

ROBERTS, FRANK H. H., JR.
    1935 A Folsom Complex. *Smithsonian Miscellaneous Collections,* Vol. 94. No. 4. Washington.
    1936 Additional Information on the Folsom Complex. *Smithsonian Miscellaneous Collections,* Vol. 95, No. 10. Washington.

ROUSE, IRVING
    1939 Prehistory in Haiti. *Yale University Publications in Anthropology,* No. 21. New Haven.
    1960 The Classification of Artifacts in Archaeology. *American Antiquity,* Vol. 25, No. 3, pp. 313-23. Salt Lake City.

SACKETT, JAMES R.
    1966 Quantitative Analysis of Upper Paleolithic Stone Tools. In "Recent Studies in Paleoanthropology," edited by J. Desmond Clark and F. Clark Howell, pp. 356-94. *Special Publication of the American Anthropological Association,* Vol. 68, No. 2, Pt. 2. Menasha.

SAHLINS, MARSHALL D. and ELMAN R. SERVICE, eds.
    1960 *Evolution and Culture.* The University of Michigan Press, Ann Arbor.

SELLARDS, ELIAS H.
    1952 *Early Man in America.* The University of Texas Press, Austin.

SEMENOV, S. A.
    1964 *Prehistoric Technology.* Barnes and Noble, New York.

SERVICE, ELMAN R.
    1962 *Primitive Social Organization.* Random House, New York.

SODAY, FRANK J.
    1954. The Quad Site, A Paleo-Indian Village in Northern Alabama. *The Tennessee Archaeologist,* Vol. 10, No. 1, pp. 1-20. Knoxville.

SPAULDING, ALBERT C.
  1957 Review of "Method and Theory in American Archaeology," by Gordon R. Willey and Philip Phillips. *American Antiquity,* Vol. 23, No. 1, pp. 85-7. Salt Lake City.

  1960a The Dimensions of Archaeology. In *Essays in the Science of Culture,* edited by Gertrude E. Dole and Robert L. Carneiro, pp. 437-56. Thomas Y. Crowell, New York.

  1960b Statistical Description and Comparison of Artifact Assemblages. In "The Application of Quantitative Methods in Archaeology," edited by Robert F. Heizer and Sherbourne F. Cook, pp. 60-83. *Viking Fund Publications in Anthropology,* No. 28. New York.

STEWARD, JULIAN H.
  1938 Basin-Plateau Aboriginal Sociopolitical Groups. *Bureau of American Ethnology, Bulletin* 120, Washington.

  1955 *Theory of Culture Change.* University of Illinois Press, Urbana.

STRUEVER, STUART
  1965 Middle Woodland Culture History in the Great Lakes Riverine Area. *American Antiquity,* Vol. 31, No. 2, pp. 211-23. Salt Lake City.

TAYLOR, WILLIAM E.
  1966 An Archaeological Perspective on Eskimo Economy. *Antiquity,* Vol. 40, No. 158, pp. 114-20. Cambridge.

TAYLOR, WALTER W.
  1948 A Study of Archeology. *Memoirs of the American Anthropological Association,* No. 69. Menasha.

THOMPSON, RAYMOND H.
  1958 Modern Yucatecan Pottery Making. *Memoris of the Society for American Archaeology,* No. 15. Salt Lake City.

VAYDA, ANDREW P.
  1966 Variations in Group Structure among the Marings of New Guinea. Paper read at 65th Annual Meeting of the American Anthropological Association. Pittsburgh.

VESCELIUS, G. S.
  1960 Archeological Sampling: A Problem of Statistical Inference. In *Essays in the Science of Culture,* edited by Gertrude E. Dole and Robert L. Carneiro, pp. 457-70. Thomas Y. Crowell, New York.

WARNICA, JAMES M.
  1966 New Discoveries at the Clovis Site. *American Antiquity,* Vol. 31, No. 3, pp. 345-57. Salt Lake City.

WHITE, LESLIE
  1949 *The Science of Culture.* Farrar Straus, New York.

  1959a The Concept of Culture. *American Anthropologist,* Vol. 61, No. 2. pp. 227-51. Menasha.

  1959b *The Evolution of Culture.* McGraw-Hill, New York.

WILLEY, GORDON R. and PHILIP PHILLIPS
  1958 *Method and Theory in American Archaeology.* The University of Chicago Press, Chicago.

WILMSEN, EDWIN N.
  1968 Lithic Analysis in Paleoanthropology. *Science,* Vol. 161, No. 3845, pp. 982-7. Washington.

WITTHOFT, JOHN
  1952 A Paleo-Indian Site in Eastern Pennsylvania: An Early Hunting Culture. *Proceedings of the American Philosophical Society,* Vol. 96, No. 4, pp. 464-95. Philadelphia.

WORMINGTON, H. MARIE
  1957 Ancient Man in North America. *Denver Museum of Natural History, Popular Series,* No. 4. Denver.